D0463566

THE ART OF CHILDREN'S PICTURE BOOKS

GARLAND REFERENCE LIBRARY
OF THE HUMANITIES
(Vol. 825)

THE ART
OF CHILDREN'S
PICTURE BOOKS
A Selective Reference Guide

Sylvia S. Marantz
and
Kenneth A. Marantz

GARLAND PUBLISHING, INC. • NEW YORK & LONDON
1988

Library of Congress Cataloging-in-Publication Data

Marantz, Sylvia S.
  The art of children's picture books: a selective reference guide
/ Sylvia S. Marantz and Kenneth A. Marantz.
        p. cm. — (Garland reference library of the humanities; v.
825)
    Bibliography: p.
    Includes indexes.
    ISBN 0–8240–2745–0 (alk. paper)

    1. Reference books—Picture-books for children—Bibliography.
  2. Reference books—Children's literature—Bibliography.
  3. Reference books—Illustrated books, Children's—Bibliography.
  4. Picture-books for children—History—Bibliography.   5. Children's
literature—History and criticism—Bibliography.   6. Illustrated
books, Children's—History—Bibliography.   I. Marantz, Kenneth A.
II. Title.   III. Series.
  Z1037.1.M37   1988   [PN1009.A1]   011.62—dc19
  88–1704   CIP

Cover design by Mary Beth Brennan

Printed on acid-free, 250-year-life paper
Manufactured in the United States of America

CONTENTS

PART VII

PREFACE

This publication began at least six years ago as a search for material for another book entirely. As the notes and references accumulated, patterns began to emerge. It was then that Gary Kuris of Garland made us aware that what we were gathering might be of interest to other researchers, and we made the fatal error of agreeing to compile it.

As anyone who has attempted any bibliography on anything already knows, the task is endless. Almost every reference leads to several more. Friends mutter half-recalled titles; partial xeroxes of periodical articles surface with dates missing or blurred; promising titles yield nothing relevant but mention other possibilities; decisions on how far to pursue must be made constantly. We found ourselves snatching moments at the card catalogs of libraries as diverse as that in the Tate Museum in London or in the center of Canberra, Australia, while on other business entirely. All too often the vital page or the entire bound volume containing the relevant issue was missing. This search has proved exhausting but cannot claim to be exhaustive. Our last computer search was done in the fall of 1985, but we have included books and articles that have come to our attention as particularly relevant from 1986 and 1987 as well. As I write, someone somewhere is printing another article we will unfortunately miss. We hope that this bibliography will serve as a springboard to carry others farther and faster in their quests. We welcome the calling of omissions and additions to our attention.

Sylvia Marantz
October 1987

INTRODUCTION

With These Lights

"Which such Book, and in such a dress may (I hope) serve to entice witty children to it, that they may not conceit a torment to be in the school, but dainty fare. For it is apparent, that children (even from their infancy almost) are delighted with Pictures, and willingly please their eyes with these lights: And it will be very well worth the pains to have once brought to pass, that scare-crows may be taken away out of Wisdom's Gardens."

The Orbis Pictus,
John Amos Comenius, 1657

In the 300 years since Comenius created what has been frequently noted as "the first children's picturebook" our gardens have not yet been cleared of all scarecrows. Despite increasing attention to the illustrations in children's books in this century, most of the concerns seem to be about the shape, size, and clothing of these scarecrows rather than with speculation about their placement in the garden. For me picture books should be perceived and valued as a form of visual art, *not* literary art. To insist on valuing them as literature makes us appreciate the pictures primarily in relationship to the text, more as handmaidens than as symbols having unique personalities. In remaining textbound we fail to exploit sufficiently the visual qualities of books that Comenius astutely identified as those that cause us delight.

Humans have created pictures for thousands of years, have chosen to make visible some of the feelings and fears and desires that inhabited their psyches. They made marks on cave walls, on bones and boulders, on dried animal skins and the plaster-coated walls of their tombs. These pictures tell us stories, in other words they illuminate or illustrate dreams or lived experiences. Whether an Italian Renaissance painting depicting the adoration of the Magi or an Amerindian drawing on an animal hide of a battle with paleface soldiers, the marks made are intended to be a visual narrative. As books evolved in the Western-world pictures have also been used to help tell stories, to make specifically visual what the text could only more generally suggest.

The history of the book, like any history of a human enterprise, is a complex one that properly demands investigation of economic, political, artistic, and technological forces operating within cultures. Obviously, without the development of movable type mass production would not be possible, and without the Industrial Revolution there wouldn't be the kind of literate and relatively affluent audience for the flood of books that technology made possible. And without emancipation of the young from the world of adult work there would have been no need to create books for children. The many histories of children's literature depict an evolution from books designed to train the moral faculties, to produce the proper behavior needed in adult society, to those, toward the end of the nineteenth century, that began to understand the value of esthetic joy for youngsters, the delight that Comenius wrote of. Randolph Caldecott, rather than Comenius, properly the father of the picture book, because unlike *The Orbis Pictus,* which was an illustrated language textbook, his books partnered lively drawings with simple story texts created to entertain, not instruct. Victorian England was the cultural engine that drove this book form into our century, with Caldecott and artists like Crane and Potter at the throttle.

The initial momentum behind picture books waned as the *illustrated book* grew in importance, with such artists as Rackham and Pyle and W.C. Wyeth and Shepard producing stacks of enticing volumes. Although difficult to pinpoint the exact year, it was sometime during the churning decades between the World Wars that the picture book regained the vitality of the earlier Golden Age, an energy that exploded into a second gilded, if not 18-carat gold, age of productivity. It is the "nowness" of this productivity with its profound unrealized potential that continues to stimulate our curiosity, to provoke our speculations about these art objects. These inquiries have, over a score of years, helped identify characteristic qualities of the genre that make it possible to be more constructively critical than most current writers have been.

One must begin with a point of view, a psychological set, a conscious frame of reference. When one goes to an art museum, one is prepared to respond to the objects as if they were whatever you may define as "art" objects. In a real sense we create "rules" for appreciating them that are different from those we use for responding to other sets of objects, for example, tools, automobiles, postage stamps. Therefore it is important to be as clear as possible about what sort of thing a picture book is. To sort it out from other related things it might be useful to imagine a line that has at one end a typical novel, that is, a book whose pages are filled exclusively with the printed word. At the other end of this imaginary line is the totally textless book, one that conveys its message (mainly a story) using only pictures. In between are volumes that have a single illustration (a frontispiece), some that employ chapter-heading or concluding vignettes, others that provide occasional full-page pictures that highlight particular events or delineate characters in the narrative, and a few that interlard a variety of illustrations throughout the entire book. In all of these examples it is possible to remove all the pictures and be left with a coherent, completely satisfying piece of literature. Artists like Doré, Picasso, Matisse, Eichenberg, Moser, Shahn, and Baskin have all contributed drawings, etchings, and woodcuts to illustrate poems and stories. Indeed, the history of the book is replete with examples of illustrated works, and, of course, the practice continues.

In responding to these kinds of books we have been conditioned by our cultural conventions to read the texts as literature, with its appropriate critical criteria, and to appreciate the visual art separately, as individual esthetic objects. It has become common practice for collectors to remove the pictures from some of these works and treat them as one would any other picture from an artist's studio: to mat, frame, and hang them on the wall. They do not lose artistic value by being separated from the text they illustrated.

In recent years a parallel practice has evolved to treat the "original" studio products of picture book artists in the same way. If the artist created a series of watercolor paintings as illustrations for a retelling of a traditional fable, for example, each one could be matted, framed, and hung on the wall. But in this case what is displayed is the fragment of something, as when a broken head of a marble statue is mounted for exhibition in a museum. The painting and the head surely have qualities that may evoke esthetic responses, but they are still incomplete; they have been removed from the context of their original design. A picture book, unlike an illustrated book, is properly conceived of as a unit, a totality that integrates all the designed parts in a sequence in which the relationships among them—the cover, endpapers, typography, pictures—are crucial to understanding the book. In a significant sense each book, like each etching pulled from the artist's copper plate, is an original artwork. All that preceded its printing, and there are many steps in the process, are but means to that end.

Therefore to appreciate a picture book one must take a point of view that is based on an understanding of it as the composite set of qualities that differentiates it from other objects. However, to complicate matters a bit, within the family of "picture books" there are several relatives that skew this viewpoint. There are collections of poems and fables whose organizational logic is quite different from that of a single story. Similarly those collections of notions ("concepts") like colors or tools or wildflowers do not have as structured a framework as a narrative demands. Alphabets and counting books may or may not have such a framework, depending on the organizing principle or their generation, but they do have a sequential logic based on their definitions as linguistic or numerical components. Then there are the collections of puzzles and fact books that tell how things work or take us into the fields to learn about nature. All have in common the twin narratives in the form of words and pictures that characterize the picture book.

All picture books tell stories. And all stories began as things told by a storyteller. When transcribed onto the silent page the voice is lost and with it the idiosyncratic manner each teller has in making the story special. The illustrator replaces the speaker and the pictures become, symbolically, the voice that conveys some of the special qualities of meaning that language frequently cannot. Conjure up images of the many mice who have been the central characters of picture books as an example of how the artist's vision can take a word—"mouse"—and create brave leaders, artistic speakers, and orators by the use of line and color. In evaluating picture books we attend to the qualities of that symbolic voice just as we attend to the "interpretation" by the vocalist or group of yet another performance of a popular musical composition. What makes that rendition special and how does it affect us?

Because the picture book is much more a visual art object than a piece of literature, book selection should focus more on the visual attributes than on the text. Clearly I must hedge this statement, because storyline, even in a textless work, is important, and, indeed, separates the routine from the seductive book. Yet picture books are such rich repositories of visual art, so readily available compared with the resources housed in galleries and museums, that I believe we must take the fullest advantage of them. Probably the most immediate quality of a picture book is its craftsmanship. Are you convinced by the way figures are rendered that they can do the things asked of them? This is not at all a matter of naturalism. Lionni's use of relatively simple cut-paper shapes to create birds and mice and alligators is very convincing. Although at times we may admire the patterned papers he uses, we look through the means of production and become believers in the reality of his characters, just as we do when we take Sendak's magic sailboat to visit the "Wild Things." In picking books you want those that can carry you beyond the surface recognition of medium and the naming of objects represented into the spiritual realm of the story.

What I am referring to here is the expressive content of the book, the stuff of effect that deals more with the "how" of communication than the "what." Beyond the bare bones of plot, how are details used in the illustrations to add a texture, even a subplot, so that the eye looks for clues in later pages based on earlier visual hints? Knight's *Twelve Days of Christmas* interweaves the escapades of a raccoon into the classical rhyme to supplement the main character's playing out of the text's events. The effect is to add even more fun to a lively retelling (i.e., visual interpretation). Color manipulates our emotions as a puppeteer's strings move a marionette's limbs. Shulevitz's changing shades of blue in his *Dawn* create major mood shifts hardly hinted at in the text. And unusual angles are devices used by Van Allsburg in drawing us into his surreal worlds. Such artistic tools are available to all, but only some illustrators think to use them.

Although it is tempting to rely on formal rules for evaluating picture books, to create canons of picturemaking and design in order to categorize and then measure each work, to do so would sap the vital juices of personal response. Most of current reviewing, however, not only avoids this deathtrap but also sidesteps the necessary attention to those qualities that contribute to the esthetic impact of the book. As a visual narrative one should expect to find humor, pathos, excitement, mystery, beauty, repulsion—the expressive content that one picks up a book to get. There is a layer of meaning that Anthony Browne instills into his version of *Hansel and Gretel* when he depicts the mother and witch looking very much alike. Further, his use of vertical elements throughout is a symbolic motif that acts upon our subconscious to add further texture to the visual meanings of the tale. The audacity of setting the piece in modern times forces us to deal with the content in nontraditional ways. These are examples of an artist consciously packing his work with clues that we must unpack if we are to derive more than a superficial reading. The "what" of the story remains basically within the traditional track. But it is "how" he goes about visualizing it, that is, creating the visual narrative, that makes all the difference. Of course there is no reason to believe that one must like a picture book after the unpacking has been done. Taste remains one of the most personal rights we have.

As with any art form, response (call it appreciation or evaluation or even criticism) is a complex affair that demands experience to make it a personal value. Because so many of us have been raised to perceive books as temples of the word, our visual-art sensibilities have not had a decent chance to develop. The sorts of analyses suggested above are not automatic and, as simple as they seem, can only hint at the extensive opportunities that picture books offer. They are available for all to become involved with, to learn from, and, hence, to enjoy. And many books have been created to help those who desire to become educated.

I am one with Comenius when he writes that "it will be very well worth the pains to have once brought to pass" the involvement with the picture books that can so delight not only "witty children" but all of us.

The Art of Children's Picture Books

PART I

History of Children's Picture Books

1. Adams, Bess Porter. *About Books and Children: Historical Survey of Children's Literature.* New York: Holt, 1953. 573pp.

   Pages 363–83 give history of illustrations in children's books through Howard Pyle, plus a few b & w reproductions. Some notes on illustrations occur *passim.*

2. Alderson, Brian. *Sing a Song for Sixpence: The English Picture Book Tradition and Randolph Caldecott.* Cambridge, Eng: Cambridge University, 1986. 112pp.

   Profusely illustrated in b & w and color. Prepared on the occasion of an exhibit at the British Library (October, 1986–January, 1987) on the centennial of Caldecott's death to "place his work within the tradition of narrative illustration" and show his role in the "English style" of picture books. Notes on woodcuts and other techniques of historic illustration, on Hogarth, Blake, Rowlandson, Cruikshank, Bennett and Evans. Discussion of Caldecott and his work begins on p. 79. Homage and examples from illustrators who followed him are on pp. 84–106.

3. Arnold, Arnold. *Pictures and Stories from Forgotten Children's Books.* New York: Dover, 1969. 169pp.

   Chiefly 485 b & w illustrations. Pages 1–8 give history of children's literature and the attempts to change it. Sections on "morals and manners," "nursery rhymes," "street cries," "fairy tales," "anthropomorphism," "Robinsonads," "humor and riffles," "books on sports, games and pastimes," "periodicals" and "books that teach" have brief explanatory introductions before the reproductions of words and pictures.

4.   Bader, Barbara. *American Picture Books from Noah's Ark to the Beast Within.* New York: Macmillan, 1976. 615pp.

Prodigious in its scope, impressive in its scholarship, yet a delightfully readable history. Chapters are sometimes devoted to significant illustrators (Wanda Gag, Dr. Seuss, Maurice Sendak); sometimes to subject matter (of the American Indian; Negro identification, Black Identity); to stylistic changes (the Dynamics and Fun of the Form, the Japanese Advent); and sometimes to the effects of cultural conditions (the American Line, Social Change, Foreign Background). 663 reproductions (130 in color) provide visual examples for her critical analysis. Without a doubt the major reference to use for a sense of the sweep of the American scene up to the mid 1970's.

5.   Barr, John. *Illustrated Children's Books.* London: British Library, 1986. 80pp.

A brief but sharply perceptive 200-year history of English publications from Newbery to Rackham. Specially valuable for its attention to the techniques of reproduction and their influence on style. Carefully and fully illustrated with b & w and full color reproductions.

6.   Barry, Florence. *A Century of Children's Books.* New York: George H. Doran, 1923. 257pp.

A British history from chap-books on.

7.   Bator, Robert, ed. *Masterworks of Children's Literature; Volumes Three and Four: The Middle Period, 1740–1836.* New York: Stonehill Publishing with Chelsea House, 1983. 2 vols.

Complete texts with some b & w illustrations for historic study.

8. Bingham, Jane. *Fifteen Centuries of Childrens' Literature: An Annotated Chronology of British and American Works in Historical Contexts.* Westport, Connecticut: Greenwood, 1980. 540pp.

Must look under individual name of author or illustrator. A straight chronology. Concise listing of major works. Short essays on each century.

9. Bland, David. *A History of Book Illustrations: The Illuminated Manuscript and the Printed Book.* Berkeley: University of California, 1969. 459pp.

Profusely illustrated (436 illustrations) in b & w and color. Begins with Egyptian papyrus, codex—continues with medieval and oriental illumination. From introduction of printing to 1520 country-by-country, from 1520–1600 country-by-country, 18th century country-by-country, 19th century country-by-country, and 20th century country-by-country.
Children's books discussed in each period and country. Information well indexed. Includes Poland, Russia, etc.

10. Boston Museum of Fine Arts. *The Artist and the Book 1860–1960, in Western Europe and the United States.* Cambridge, Mass.: Harvard University and the Boston Museum of Fine Arts, 1961. Catalog of an exhibition.

Children's books barely represented since more celebrated artists, especially painters and sculptors, "seldom touched them."

11. Bravo-Villasante, Carmen. *Historia de la Literatura Infantil Espanola.* Madrid: Revista de Occidente, 1959. 270pp.

Includes magazines for children (pp. 75–86). Some illustrations reproduced in color.

12. Brenni, Vito, J., comp. *Book Illustration and Decoration: A Guide to Research.* Westport, Connecticut: Greenwood, 1980. 191pp.

Includes sections on reference works, book decoration, manuals of illustration and other writings on technique (e.g., etching, lithography, color printing), history of methods of illustration, from ancient times to present (general and by time period, in individual countries) science and technology, medicine, music, geography and history. Part 7, "Illustration and decoration in children's books," pp. 121–136, includes art, techniques and principles; pp. 121–122, early history to 1900; pp.123–124, twentieth century; pp. 124–126 and in individual counties pp. 126–136. Includes references to early sources not repeated in this bibliography.

13. Butler, Francelia, ed. *Masterworks of Children's Literature, Volumes One and Two: The Early Years, 1550–1739.* New York: Stonehill Publishing with Chelsea House, 1983. 2 vols.

Complete versions of the texts of selected works, with some b & w illustrations.

14. Caradec, Francois. *Histoire de la Litterature Enfantine en France.* Paris: Albin Michel, 1877. 271pp.

Discusses history of children's literature in France with references to some other countries as well. Pp. 129–139 cover illustrators.

15. Cott, Jonathan, gen. ed. *Masterworks of Children's Literature.* See editors of individual volumes: Francelia Butler, *The Early Years, 1550–1739*; Robert Bator, *The Middle Period, 1740–1836*; Robert Lee Wolff, *The Victorian Age, 1837–1900*; Jonathan Cott, *Victorian Color Picture Books*; William T. Moynihan, and Mary E. Shaner, *The Twentieth Century.*

16. _____, gen. ed. *Masterworks of Children's Literature, Volume Seven: Victorian Color Picture Books.* New York: Stonehill Publishing with Chelsea House, 1983. 184pp.

Selections of text and color illustrations from works of Caldecott, Crane, Greenaway, Doyle, Ballantyne and others. "A Dialogue with Maurice Sendak," pp. IX–XXI has detailed criticism of the artists and works included.

17. Crane, Walter. *Of the Decorative Illustration of Books Old and New*. London: Bracken, 1896, 1984. 243pp.

Many b & w illustrations. Crane's historic account of book design and illustration and what he considers a "revival" of printing as an art. His comments on children's books, pp. 126–132 include toy books.

18. Darton, Frederick J. Harvey. *Children's Books in England: Five Centuries of Social Life*. Cambridge, Eng.: Cambridge University, 1932. 1958 (2nd ed.). 3rd edition with extensive revisions by Brian Alderson, 1982. 398pp.

Some b & w illustrations. Although he does not deal with picture books specifically or at length, he does include them in his historic survey. His comments on them and the processes used for them can be found through the index under "illustration" and "illustrations."

19. De Vries, Leonard. *Flowers of Delight*. New York: Pantheon Books, 1965. 232pp. From the Osborne Collection of Early Children's Books.

"An agreeable garland of prose and poetry for the instruction and amusement of little masters and misses and their distinguished parents. Embellished with some 700 elegant woodcuts and engravings on wood and copper of which upwards of 125 are neatly colored. Selected with the greatest care from books for juvenile minds, 1765–1830." Includes a note on the Osborne collection in Toronto, an anthologist's note on the history of children's books, some notes on the original books and on the writers, illustrators and publishers. Bibliography.

20. Doyle, Brian, ed. *The Who's Who of Children's Literature*. New
     York: Schocken, 1968. 380pp.

     104 plates of b & w illustrations. Emphasis is on the English-
     language authors and early classics from 1800–1968. "The
     illustrators" (pp. 304–357) is an alphabetical dictionary of
     illustrators from Tenniel to Wildsmith with biographical
     information and their chief works listed. Medal winners are
     included.

21. *Early Children's Books and Their Illustration*. New York:
     Pierpont Morgan Library, and Boston: David R. Godine, 1975.
     263pp.

     Illustrated in b & w and color with facsimile pages and
     illustrations. Beginning with historical background, 225
     outstanding examples of these books have been chosen from the
     library's collection to be discussed by type (Aesop's Fables,
     ABC's, primers, etc.) including comments on the illustration.
     Separate chapters cover Edward Lear, pp. 242–246, and Beatrix
     Potter, pp. 247–249. Other illustrators are accessible from the
     Index; e.g., Kate Greenaway.

22. Feaver, William. *When We Were Young: Two Centuries of
     Children's Book Illustration*. New York: Holt, 1977. 96pp.

     Chiefly color and b & w illustrations. A comprehensive
     international survey of techniques, sources, influences and styles
     of the best-known illustrators from William Blake to Maurice
     Sendak.

23. Field, Louise Frances (Story). *The Child and His Book: Some
     Account of the History and Progress of Children's Literature in
     England*. London: W. Gardner, Darton and Co., 1891. 1892 (2nd
     ed.). Reissued Detroit: Singing Tree, Book Tower, 1968. 358pp.

     A few b & w illustrations. Includes history from "Before the
     Norman Conquest," and a discussion of the life of the child.
     Chapter XIV, "Some illustrators of children's books," pp. 293–

315 discusses the early illustrators from Bewick to the author's time. A very interesting comparison is drawn between the "too good" results of the improved technology and the "directness and simplicity of the older illustrations," and the effect on the reader.

24. Fraser, James, H. *Society and Children's Literature: Papers Presented on Research, Social History, and Children's Literature.* Sponsored by the School of Library Science, Simmons College, and the Committee on National Planning for the Special Collections of the Children's Services Division of the American Library Association. May 14–15, 1976. Boston: Godine, 1978. 209pp.

Chapter 9, "Manuscripts of Children's Literature in the Beinecke Library" by Marjorie G. Wynne, pages 139–149, includes descriptions of the letters of Edward Lear with illustrations, many works of Walter Crane, and Arthur Rackham's original illustrations for *Peter Pan in Kensington Gardens* in the collection at Yale.

25. Georgiou, Constantine. *Children and Their Literature.* Englewood Cliffs, New Jersey: Prentice-Hall, 1969. 501pp.

Includes some b & w illustrations. Chapter 2, pp. 15–43, is a history of children's books. Chapter 4, pp. 61–105, "Picture books and story books," discusses Nursery Rhymes, alphabet and counting books, concept books, books for easy reading, and books on other cultures. Lists criteria, including design, but does not spend much time discussing or analyzing the illustrations. His annotations for his list of books include mention and description of illustrations.

26. Gobels, Hubert. *Hundert Alte Kinderbucher 1870–1945: Eine Illustrierte Bibliographie.* Germany: Harenberg, 1981. 436pp.

Contains a page of information on each book, a reproduction in b & w of the title page and two more pages reproduced in b & w, usually of illustrations. "Nachwort," pp. 411–430.

27.   Harthan, John. *The History of the Illustrated Book, The Western Tradition*. London: Thames and Hudson, 1981. 465pp.

      33 of the pages are in color. For general historic background, some children's book illustrators are mentioned such as Quentin Blake on p. 279, and Sendak, Macaulay and Chwast on pp. 280–281, and examples of the work of others are included.

28.   Haviland, Virginia, and Margaret N. Coughlan, eds. *Yankee Doodle's Literary Sampler of Prose, Poetry and Pictures: Being an Anthology of Diverse Works Published for the Edification and/or Entertainment of Young Readers in America before 1900*. Selected from the Rare Book Collections of the Library of Congress. New York: Thomas Crowell, 1974. 466pp.

      A brief introduction followed by reproductions of the books. Bibliography.

29.   Hewins, Caroline Maria. *A Mid-Century Child and Her Books*. New York: Macmillan, 1926. Detroit: Singing Tree, 1969. 136pp.

      Some small b & w illustrations. Describes her childhood and the books she remembers from the late 19th century, with some comments on the pictures. A reproduction of an old alphabet, pp. 123–136.

30.   Huck, Charlotte S., with Susan Hepler and Janet Hickman. *Children's Literature in the Elementary School*. 4th ed. New York: Holt, Rinehart and Winston, 1987. 753pp.

      Illustrated in b & w and color. All editions of this book have chapters on the history of children's books and on picture books, their art and artists. Chapter 3, "Changing world of children's books," pp. 94–142, covers the history here. Chapter 5, "Picture books," pp. 195–249, including a multi-page color insert of illustrations, covers a definition, the art and the artists, the language, the content, guides for evaluation, and themes and subjects.

31. Hurlimann, Bettina. *Three Centuries of Children's Books in Europe.* Translated and edited by Brian W. Alderson. Cleveland: World Publishing Co., 1967. 297pp.

Some b & w and color illustrations and photographs. This comprehensive historical picture includes: Chapter 10, "Education through pictures," pp. 127–144, covers the history of pictures in books. Chapter 11, pp. 145–151, "Photography," discusses this type of illustration briefly. Chapter 12, "Colour prints," pp. 152–159, covers the historic addition of color. Chapter 13, "Wham! Sok! Thinks!," pp. 160–172, is comic strips from Wilhelm Busch to Walt Disney. Chapter 15, "Jean de Brunhoff," pp, 195–200. Chapter 16, "Picture books in the twentieth century," pp. 201–245, covers books from all countries and their production.

32. *Illustrators of Children's Books.* Published yearly in conjunction with the Bologna International Children's Bookfair.

Catalog of invited artists with example of work and biographical information.

33. *Images a la Page: Une Histoire de l'Image dans les Livres pour l'Enfants.* Paris: Gallimard, 1984. 128pp.

In conjunction with two exhibitions in Paris in 1984 and 1985, a group of writers have summarized the history of children's book illustration, with emphasis on France, and have discussed current changes in technology and their effects on the art and artists of today. Authors include Jean Claverie, Christiane Clerc, Etienne Delessert, Catherine Gendrin, Claude Lapointe, Yves Lebrun, Laura Noesser, Claude-Ann Parmegiani, Patrick Roegiers, Roland Topor, François Vie.
A list of illustrators currently active, with their works, is appended.

34. International Board On Books For Young People. Section française. *Dictionnaire des Ecrivains pour la Jeunesse: Auteurs de la Langue Français.* Paris: Seghers, 1969. 214pp.

A dictionary-like list of authors with their dates, brief notes, list of their works, including a few illustrators. List of prize winners.

35.   Johnson, Diana L. *Fantastic Illustration and Design in Britain, 1850–1930.* With an essay by George P. Landow. Providence: Rhode Island School of Design, Museum of Art, 1979. 240pp.

Chiefly illustration, some in color. Catalog for exhibition at Museum and at Cooper-Hewitt Museum of the Smithsonian. Essay, pp. 9–27, discusses the nature and role of fantastic illustration and design and its relation to the political and social life of the times as well as the artistic climate. The relationship between children's literature and fantasy and how the world of imagination in childhood is carried into maturity is discussed on pp. 15–16. Realms of literary fancy are covered, pp. 28–43. A list of items on exhibit with information on the object and the artist, if known, follows to p. 97. The rest of the book consists of plates.

36.   Jones, Linda Harris. *A Comparison of the Works of Walter Crane, Randolph Caldecott and Kate Greenaway and Their Contributions to Children's Literature.* Chapel Hill: University of North Carolina, 1965. 57pp.

Thesis for M.S. in Library Science. Following a brief historical summary, Jones summarizes the life and the work of Crane, pp. 9–23, Caldecott, pp. 24–29, and Greenaway, pp. 30–38, with some analysis of the style of individual works. Chapter V, "Comparisons of the characteristics of the artists' work," pp. 39–46, finds many similarities in both their lives and their work. Chapter VI, pp. 47–52, shows Jones' appreciation of their contributions to the field of children's book illustration, including a discussion of children's preference studies. The bibliography includes works not covered in this selected bibliography.

37.   Lewis, John. *The Twentieth Century Book.* New York: Van Nostrand Reinhold, 1967. 270pp.

Profusely illustrated in b & w and color. Chapter 7, pp. 176–241, deals with "the illustration and design of children's books." After a review of the popular books and illustrators of the late 19th century (adventures, fairy tales, Beatrix Potter) Lewis moves to the acceptance of the three- and four-color half-tones at the start of the 20th century. The French added a "new look" in color lithography with Boutet de Monvel and others. Lewis discusses other artists such as de Brunhoff, Artzybasheff, Ardizzone, and new editions of classics. Page 216 begins "the graphic designer's book," including a discussion of Ben Shahn. Finally, he discusses the design of books for schools.

38. Lystad, Mary. *From Dr. Mather to Dr. Seuss: 200 Years of American Books for Children.* Boston: Hall, 1980. 264pp.

Despite 50 b & w reproductions of illustrations from all periods, it is remarkable in its lack of attention to illustration, illustrators and picture books. There is no index and there is no reference to this in the table of contents. Includes social history and changing social values for children.

39. MacDonald, Ruth K. *Literature for Children in England and America from 1646 to 1774.* Troy, New York: Whitston, 1982. 204pp.

Several cogent remarks (twelve, approx.) about key people and books. Helps explain the role of pictures, qualities, techniques.

40. Madura, Nancy L. "The Impact of Phototechnology on the Illustrations in Picturebooks." M.A. Thesis, Ohio State University, Columbus, 1986. 93pp.

An exploration of the Victorian period's incorporations of the newly invented photographic reproduction capabilities as they affected the works of such illustrators as Crane, Greenaway, Potter, Dulac, etc. A summary timeline superimposes Processes, Inventions, Publications and Illustrators.

41. Mahony, Bertha E.; Louise Payson Latimer; and Beulah
     Folmsbee, compilers. *Illustrators of Children's Books, 1744–
     1945*. Boston: Horn Book, 1947. 527pp.

     Contains many small and full-page b & w illustrations. Part I,
     "History and development," includes articles on the history of
     children's books, on 19th-century British illustrators, on early
     American illustration, on "Howard Pyle and His Times" by
     Robert Lawson, pp. 103–122, on foreign picture books, on
     graphic processes, illustrators, animation, 20th-century develop-
     ments, and "The Book Artist: Yesterday and Tomorrow" by Lynd
     Ward, pp. 247–262. Part III, "Biographies," gives a dictionary
     listing of living illustrators with a paragraph of biographical
     information, names of works, and in some cases, quotations. Part
     IV, "Appendix," gives a bibliography of sources for each chapter
     of each section.

42. ————, and Elinor Whitney. *Contemporary Illustrators of
     Children's Books*. Boston: Bookshop for Boys and Girls, 1930.
     Gale reprint, 1978.

     Alphabetical listing of illustrators with a paragraph or two of
     bio-bibliographic information, some provided by the person; also
     criticism quoted. Small b & w illustrations throughout. Final
     section contains essays on types of illustrated children's literature
     in Germany and France, introduction on illustration by Lynd Ward
     and essays on past influences: "The Bewicks: Thomas and John"
     by Wilbur Macy Stone, pp. 99–100. "The Fairies Come Into
     Their Own" (on Cruikshank, Doyle, Tenniel and Hughes) by
     Jacqueline Overton, pp. 101–109. "Tuppence Colored" (on Crane,
     Caldecott and Greenaway) by Jacquelene Overton, pp. 110–125.
     "The Brandywine Tradition: Howard Pyle and N.C. Wyeth" by
     Dudley Cammett Lunt, pp. 126–130. "About Lovat Fraser" by
     Rachel Field, pp. 131–132.

43. McCulloch, Lou. *Children's Books of the 19th Century*.
     Photographic illustrations by Thomas R. McCulloch. Des
     Moines: Wallace-Homestead, 1979. 152pp.

"An informative reference with prices, tracing the early history of children's books." Has some examples in color of many types of books, with related books and current values of each.

44. McLean, Ruari. *Victorian Book Design and Colour Printing.* 2nd ed. Berkeley: University of California, 1972. 241pp.

Many b & w illustrations and 16 color plates. Larger format and different plates from earlier British edition. Includes information on the radical changes taking place at the time. Chapter 6, pp. 47–63, covers "Children's books up to 1850."

45. Meyer, Susan E. *A Treasury of the Great Children's Book Illustrators.* New York: Abrams, 1983. 271pp.

Profusely illustrated in b & w and color on almost every page. All of the illustrators discussed were born in the 19th century. The introduction gives details of the art, literature and technology of the period, and of the lives of children. Pages 9–47 compare Britain and the United States. This handsome book is as valuable for its visual as for its verbal quality.

The illustrators included are: Edward Lear, pp. 49–63; John Tenniel, pp. 65–77; Walter Crane, pp. 79–93; Randolph Caldecott, pp. 95–107; Kate Greenaway, pp. 109–125; Beatrix Potter, pp. 127–141; Ernest H. Shepard, pp. 143–155; Arthur Rackham, pp. 157–175; Edmund Dulac, pp. 177–193; Kay Nielsen, pp. 195–209; Howard Pyle, pp. 211–231; N. C. Wyeth, pp. 233–247; W.W. Denslow, pp. 249–265.

46. Morris, Charles Henry. *The Illustration of Children's Books.* London: Library Association, 1957. 18pp.

Brief summary of history and techniques, including important names, pp. 1–16, is followed by notes on "the kinds of pictures which appeal to children," pp. 16–18.

47. Moynihan, William T., and Mary E. Shaner, eds. *Masterworks of Children's Literature, Volume Eight: The Twentieth Century.*

New York: Stonehill Publishing with Chelsea House, 1983. 333pp.

Full-page b & w illustrations. Texts themselves not needed in this volume since they are readily available. Chapters summarize developments in major genres. Of particular interest: Ann Devereaux Jordan, "Small Wonders: Baby Books and Picture-books," pp. 193–220, summarizes the developments in this area and analyzes what is currently available for the very young (Baby Books) and gives a quick overview of important figures and trends in picture books.

48. Muir, Marcie. *A History of Australian Children's Book Illustration.* New York: Oxford University Press, 1982. 160pp.

Many b & w and some color examples of the illustrations amplify the text. Relates the history of Australian children's books to that of books and illustrations in general and to Australian history. Chapters cover emerging Australian illustrators, special stories for boys and for girls, books about imaginary creatures as well as those peculiar to Australia. Traces developments between the wars and their flourishing after the second world war to the present. Mostly description rather than interpretive criticism or analysis of illustrations.

49. Muir, Percy. *English Children's Books, 1600–1900.* New York: Praeger, 1954. 255pp.

Chapter 7, "The Importance of Pictures," pp. 172–204, includes the important names in picture books and illustrated books. The bibliography, pp. 192–196, is loaded with references for further study. List of books by date and artist, pp. 197–203. Technical processes, the work of Greenaway and Evans, Caldecott and Crane, are covered, with reproductions in b & w and elegant color. Chapter 8, "Nick-nacks," pp. 204–217, discusses toy books, paper dolls, etc. "Three R's," pp. 217ff, covers didactic books.

50. _____. *Victorian Illustrated Books.* New York: Praeger, 1971. 287pp.

Illustrated with b & w and a few color examples. Chapter 2: "Catnachery, chapbooks and children's books," sets the stage for the books that came later. Picture books and their illustrators are mentioned or discussed along with other illustrated books. Foreign influences, including American, are also discussed.

51. Pellowski, Anne. *The World of Children's Literature.* New York: Bowker, 1968. 538pp.

Comprehensive world-wide bibliography. Introductory essays on the state of children's literature in each area and country are followed by an annotated bibliography for that place. Access through the "Illustrations of children's books" entry in the index, country by country.

52. Peppin, Brigid. *Fantasy: The Golden Age of Fantastic Illustration.* New York: Watson-Guptill, 1975. 192pp.

Chiefly color and b & w illustrations. "Introduction," pp. 7–22, covers the artists, their work and technique. Work for children is included, from artists Walter Crane, Edmund Dulac, Rudyard Kipling, Edward Lear, Kay Nielson, Arthur Rackham, John Tenniel, and others.

53. Peterson, Linda Kauffman, and Marilyn Leathers Solt. *Newbery and Caldecott Medal and Honor Books: An Annotated Bibliography.* Boston: G.K. Hall, 1982. 427pp.

Includes history of the medals, notes on characteristics and trends. Each book is listed with summary and critical commentary. Complete list to 1981. Appendix: terms, definitions, criteria, pp. 399–401.

54. Pickering, Samuel F. *John Locke and Children's Books in Eighteenth-Century England.* Knoxville: University of Tennessee, 1981. 286pp.

Clear b & w reproductions in original size. Includes analysis of chapbooks, pp. 104–137.

55.   Pitz, Henry Clarence. *Illustrating Children's Books: History, Technique, Production.* New York: Watson-Guptill, 1963. 207pp.

Includes b & w and color illustrations. Part I, "History," pp. 13–102, begins with Comenius in the 17th century, discusses the British graphic tradition from which children's illustrators emerged, covers European developments from 1800 on, covers America from early history through Pyle and the Brandywine tradition to the artists and techniques of the mid-20th century.

Part II, "Technique and Production," begins with a division of the segments of children's books by age level and characteristics of each. He then describes the physical structure of the book and how to set up pages, discusses typography and design, and the methods of reproduction of illustrations plus the way to prepare for reproduction. Final tips are on the handling of an illustrating assignment.

56.   Poltarnees, Welleran. *All Mirrors Are Magic Mirrors: Reflections On Pictures Found In Children's Books.* La Jolla, California: Green Tiger, 1972. 60pp.

Profusely illustrated with b & w drawings and tipped-in color plates. Thoughts on the purpose of children's books, descriptions and discussion of the work of many illustrators, including Maurice Sendak, Arthur Rackham, Kate Greenaway, and others, as he treats the "Realm of faerie," the relation between pictures and words, between author and illustrator, "domestic happiness" and "looking at pictures of animals."

57.   Ray, Gordon N. *The Illustrator and the Book in England from 1790–1914.* New York: Pierpont Morgan Library, 1976. 336pp.

Profusely illustrated with chiefly b & w illustrations. Discussion of the subject is included in this catalogue for an exhibition of the author's collection at the Morgan Library in March and April, 1976. Among the illustrators whose works were in the exhibit and who have their lives and work described briefly are Edward Lear, pp. 59–62; Sir John Tenniel, pp. 116–117; Walter Crane, pp.

151–154; Randolph Caldecott, pp. 154–155; Kate Greenaway, pp. 156–157; and Arthur Rackham, pp. 203–206. Works by Beatrix Potter, Edmund Dulac and Kay Nielsen are mentioned on pp. 208–209.

58. Reed, Walt, and Roger Reed. *The Illustrator in America, 1880–1980: A Century of Illustration.* New York: Madison Square, 1984. 355pp.

Profusely illustrated, mainly color, on every page. A decade-by-decade survey listing artists with some information on their life and work. A few illustrators for children are included; e.g., Jessie Willcox Smith, N.C. Wyeth, Maurice Sendak, but the index must be searched name by name.

59. Rosenbach, A.S.W. *Early American Children's Books with Bibliographic Descriptions of the Books in his Private Collection.* New York: Dover, 1971. 354pp.

Establishes the kinds of books available to children in our history. Information on the illustrations must be derived from the individual descriptions and introduction, b & w illustrations.

60. Sale, Roger. *Fairy Tales and After: From Snow White to E.B. White.* Cambridge, Massachusetts: Harvard University Press, 1978. 280pp.

B & w illustrations. Literary analysis of some fairy tales and other children's books and their authors. Part of the discussion of Beatrix Potter concerns her art.

61. Smith, Dora V. *Fifty Years of Children's Books, 1910–1960: Trends, Backgrounds, Influences.* Champaign, Illinois: National Council of Teachers of English, 1963. 149pp.

Includes "Golden age of children's books, 1925–1940," p. 32; the American picture book, p. 34; photographic picture books, p. 37; children's books in World War II and beyond (1940–1949); the picture book, pp. 55–56; children's books in a bursting world

(1950–1960); more good picture books, pp. 67–70; Summary: the perfecting of the picture book, pp. 92–93. Many bibliographies; many small b & w reproductions.

62.   Smith, Janet Adam. *Children's Illustrated Books*. London: Collins, 1948. 50pp.

With four plates in color and 33 b & w illustrations. Gives a brief history. Covers toy books, boxes. "Illustrated Story Books" from p. 21 discusses Tenniel, MacDonald, Lear and other Victorians, then Evans making possible Crane, Greenaway and Caldecott. Page 39 begins discussion of the 20th century, Rackham, Dulac and others. Compares the best of the modern books with contemporary posters and advertising lithography.

63.   Targ, William, ed. *Bibliophile in the Nursery: A Bookman's Treasury of Collector's Lore on Old and Rare Children's Books*. Cleveland: World, 1957. 503pp.

A few b & w illustrations. Pages 468–487, "Illustrators in the Nursery," by Richard Williamson Ellis, include several paragraphs of notes on the life and works of illustrators from Caldecott, Crane, Greenaway, Pyle and Rackham to Van Loon, de Angeli, Lawson, Sewell, Pitz, Artzybasheff and Duvoisin.

64.   Thorpe, James. *English Illustration: The Nineties*. New York: Hacher Art Books, 1975. 268pp.

Illustrated with many b & w examples. Establishes the environment of general illustration in which the talents of illustrators for children flourished, including periodicals as well as books. Individual illustrators can be found through the index.

65.   Thwaite, Mary F. *From Primer to Pleasure in Reading: An Introduction to the History of Children's Books in England from the Invention of Printing to 1914 with an Outline of Some Developments in Other Countries*. Boston: The Horn Book, 1963. 340pp.

In the context of general history of children's literature, the section on "Picture books and books for young children" (pp. 188–200), covers important names. The summary of other countries includes mention of important picture books. Contains 28 pages of b & w illustrations.

66. Trignon, Jean de. *Histoire de la Litterature enfantine, de la Mere l'Oye au Roi Babar.* Paris: Hachette, 1950. 241pp.

This historic discussion includes both magazine and book illustrators, non-French (Crane, Rackham, Bilibin, Disney) and French from Boutet de Monvel on. Illustrators are accessible through the index.

67. Tuer, Andrew W. *Pages and Pictures from Forgotten Children's Books.* Originally published in London: Leadenhall, 1898–1899. Reissued, Detroit: Singing Tree, Book Tower, 1969. 510pp.

Brief introduction (pp. 5–10) which describes some of the books and how they were colored, followed by b & w reproduced pages from nearly 100 old books.

68. Wakeman, Geoffrey. *Aspects of Victorian Lithography: Anastatic Printing and Photozineography.* Wymondham, England: Brewhouse, 1970. 63pp.

Descriptions of these technical processes used for duplication of facsimiles in the 19th century. Inserted facsimiles.

69. Weinstein, Frederic D. *Walter Crane and the American Book Arts, 1880–1915.* Columbia University, 1970. D.L.S. 271pp. Useful bibliography primarily of pre-1925 references.

A thoughtful, if less than totally convincing, analysis of Cranes' influence on the design and illustration of American books. Children's books are given some special emphasis. Most useful for its total coverage of Crane's work.

70.   Weitenkampf, Frank. *The Illustrated Book*. Cambridge, Mass.:
       Harvard University, 1938. 314pp.

       Historical approach, century by century, detailing technique and
       important people and places. Gives many examples in b & w of
       whole pages with lettering and illustration. Illustrators of
       children's books not important. Chapter 10, "Color Work and
       Children's Books," (pp. 213–224) discusses the technique of color
       development especially in the 19th century in England (Crane,
       Greenaway) and other countries (Boutet de Monvel, Pyle, Parrish,
       Bilibin) and some comments on adult attitudes toward illustrations
       for children.

71.   Whalley, Joyce Irene. *Cobwebs to Catch Flies: Illustrated
       Books for the Nursery and Schoolroom 1700–1900*. Berkeley:
       University of California, 1974. 163pp.

       After a summary of the early history of pictures in books and of
       the techniques used, Whalley discusses didactic books by type:
       Alphabet, Counting, Religious Instruction, Moral Improvement,
       History, Geography and Travel, Street Cries and Occupations,
       Natural History and Science, Grammar, Music, Languages. The
       bibliography lists further books in each area for study in addition
       to books about these early books.

72.   Wolff, Robert Lee, ed. *Masterworks of Children's Literature,
       Volumes Five and Six: The Victorian Age, 1837–1900*. New
       York: Stonehill Publishing with Chelsea House, 1983. 2 vols.

       Texts of historic interest. See Volume Seven edited by Jonathon
       Cott for the Color Picture Books of this period.

PART II

How a Picture Book is Made

73. Aliki. *How a Book Is Made.* New York: Crowell, 1986. 32pp.

A picture book for children which details the steps in the production of a picture book from the idea in the head of the author to the arrival in the bookstore. Shows the role of the editor, artist, designer, copyeditor, typesetter, proofreader, production director. Details how the art is reproduced and the other steps of printing and production.

74. Althea (Althea Braithwaite). *Making a Book.* Cambridge, England: Dinosaur, 1980. Unpaginated.

This picture book for children simply and succinctly describes how a typical book is produced, from typesetting to bookshop.

75. Colby, Jean Poindexter. *Writing, Illustrating and Editing Children's Books.* New York: Hastings House, 1967. 318 pp.

Includes some b & w photographs, diagrams and illustrations. Part I discusses writing. Part II, pp. 91–207, discusses illustration and production. The qualities that are necessary for each age group through high school are listed and defined with examples. Requirements for the illustrator may be outdated by current technology. Includes setting fees and getting started. Pages 131–148 give a timetable for a picture book, what really happens in the course of producing the book among all those concerned (editor, production manager, printer) from start to printing; pp. 149–172 discuss typography and book design with examples; pp. 173–186 detail printing methods; pp. 187–198 discuss binding and jackets, also with examples; pp. 199–208: "Production close calls: what can go terribly wrong." Part III, "Editing," is of general interest. Covers awards and the Children's Book Council.

76.   *Evolution of a Graphic Concept: The Stonecutter.* (Sound Filmstrip.) Weston, Connecticut: Weston Woods, 1977. 1 Filmstrip, 1 Cassette. 71 frames, 15 min.

The artist, Gerald McDermott, describes his background and his choice of this tale to film and then to illustrate. His research, step-by-step process of development, including decisions made, and all steps of the art work are described and shown.

77.   *Gail E. Haley: Wood and Linoleum Illustration.* (Sound Filmstrip.) Weston, Connecticut: Weston Woods, 1978. 1 Filmstrip, 1 Cassette. 72 frames, 17 min.

The artist herself tells something of the history of printmaking. Then she uses her work for *A Story A Story* as an example to show how she evolved her illustrations from her inspirations in African art, how she did the illustrations from drawings and joined paper figures through linoleum blocks and watercolor painting.

78.   Garrett, Caroline S.   "A Fairytale Book: Exploration into Creating an Art Form." M.A. Thesis, Ohio State University, Columbus, 1985. 68pp.

Evolution of a theory of fairytales and the testing of the relationship of text and illustration through the creation of an illustrated original story.

79.   Gates, Frieda. *How to Write, Illustrate and Design Children's Books.* Monsey, New York: Lloyd-Simone, 1986. 155pp.

An up-to-date, comprehensive manual full of practical wisdom. Sections include a very brief history, analysis of categories of books, details of techniques and media, specifications for step-by-step production, marketing procedures and contract advice. The 276 b & w illustrations and 53 color reproductions provide crucial information. An elaborate glossary is useful in defining the many technical terms.

80. Gordon, Stephan F. *Making Picture-Books: A Method of Learning Graphic Sequence.* New York: Van Nostrand Reinhold, 1970. 96pp.

Chiefly b & w illustration. Discusses subject, style, theme, page design, materials and gives examples, not necessarily for children's books. Especially good for the demonstrating of the sequential techniques, beyond just the design of individual pages, needed for picture books.

81. Greenfeld, Howard. *Books from Writer to Reader.* New York: Crown, 1976. 211pp.

B & w and color examples of illustrations. Clear analysis of literary agent, publishing house, role of the editor, how an illustrator prepares work for publication, what the copy editor, designer, jacket designer, production supervisor, compositor, proofreader and indexer do, how the book is printed including how colorwork is done, the binding, the trip from publisher to warehouse to bookstore, and, finally, the publicity and reviews that bring it to the attention of the reader. Glossary.

82. Gross, Gerald, ed. *Editors on Editing.* Rev. ed. New York: Harper and Row, 1985. 373pp.

In addition to information on all kinds of editing, it also contains: Ann Beneduce, "Planting Inflammatory Ideas in the Garden of Delight: Relections on Editing Children's Books," pp. 258–264 which includes some comments on picture books and their makers.

83. Hands, Nancy S. *Illustrating Children's Books: A Guide to Drawing, Printing, and Publishing.* Englewood Cliffs, N.J.: Prentice-Hall, 1986. 166pp.

Some b & w illustrations and a four-page color insert. Provides useful examples in this manual for would-be illustrators. The writing is simple with frequent exercises, questions and practical advice to assist the user. Chapters cover such logical topics as "Looking at Artists at work," "Types of Children's Books," "Preparing Art for Printing," and "Publishing." A glossary and four pages of Resources and a brief history of illustrated books are useful supplements.

84. *How a Picture Book is Made: The Making of the Island of the Skog from Conception to Finished Book.* (Sound Filmstrip, 66 frames: 10 min.) Weston, Connecticut: Weston Woods, 1976.

Steven Kellogg tells how he became a picture book artist. He describes, from first ideas to printed book in hand, all the steps taken and people involved in the production of his picture book.

85. Jacques, Robin. *Illustrators at Work.* London: Studio Books, 1963. 112pp.

Although only a few children's book artists are included among the succinct biographies in this practical reference, the sections on the historical influences and technical information of "processes of reproduction" and the business of illustration provide relevant insights. This book is limited to b & w artists working "in the main English illustrative tradition." Over 70 illustrations.

86. Jensen, Virginia Allen. "A Picturebook for the Blind." *Bookbird* (January, 1980): 7–12.

An account of the creation of *What's That*, a picture book for blind youngsters, much on the technical problems of printing a book that appeals to all sorts of children and can be produced economically.

87. Kehoe, Michael. *The Puzzle of Books.* Minneapolis: Carolrhoda, 1982. Unpaginated.

B & w photographs on every page of this children's book make clear the people and the operations involved in the making of a particular book from the arrival of the author's manuscript at the editor's desk through the work of the artist, designer, typesetter, keyliner, camera person, stripper, platemaker, printer, and binder to produce the book for library or bookstore.

88. Kurth, Heinz. *Print a Book.* Baltimore: Penguin, 1975. 32pp.

A picture book for children which discusses the production process, shows tone block and color separation, and finally encourages the reader to make a flip-book, giving full instructions.

89. Lucas, Barbara. "Picture Books for Children Who are Masters of Few Words." *School Library Journal* 19 (May, 1973): 31–35 and *Library Journal* 98 (May 15, 1973): 1641–1645.

In showing why picture books "cost so much" Lucas details how a book is made, including the role of the editor and some of the costs of color processes, paper, etc.

*   Pitz, Henry Clarence. *Illustrating Children's Books: History, Technique, Production.* Cited above as item 55.

90. Ryder, John. *The Case for Legibility.* New York: Moretus, 1979. 77pp.

Profusely illustrated with b & w examples and diagrams. Discusses how the design of a book can aid in its legibility, with the various steps to be taken, the choices to be made; i.e., typeface, paper, margins, spaces up to jacket design.

91. Shulevitz, Uri. *Writing with Pictures: How to Write and Illustrate Children's Books.* New York: Watson-Guptill, 1985. 271pp.

Profusely illustrated in b & w and color. Large and handsomely designed. Part I defines picture books and story books and shows actual story telling picture sequences, good and poor, and defines elements of story and refining it. Part II begins with storyboard and dummy. Elements of size, shape, and scale are shown with many examples, as are the parts of a book from jacket to sewing. Part III, "Creating the Pictures," gives examples and contrasts others to show the purpose of illustration (decoration, expressiveness, etc.). Lessons in drawing figures and objects include examples of many kinds and demonstrate how to use references sources, including nature, for some details. Notes on elements of composition also include many examples. Drawing techniques are demonstrated, as are steps toward a personal style. Part IV details steps necessary to prepare art work for reproduction, including the nature of the printing process, color preparation, and examples from his own work on different techniques to reproduce for the effect desired.

92.   Stan, Susan. "Conversations: Susan Hirschman." *The Five Owls* 2, no. 1 (September–October, 1987): 7.

B & w photographs. Brief summaries of how the editor at Greenwillow works with the artist/author, especially her experiences with alphabet books.

93.   Stone, Bernard, and Arthur Eckstein. *Preparing Art for Printing.* Rev. ed. New York: Van Nostrand Reinhold, 1983. 194pp.

Profusely illustrated in b & w and color. A detailed explanation of the processes of modern commercial printing and how the graphic artist must work with them to prepare artwork for printing. Includes tools and equipment and covers one-color and multi-color printing. All terms are explained in detail.

94.   *Story of a Book.* (Sound Filmstrip.) Verdurgo City, California: Pied Piper, 1970. 1 Filmstrip, 1 cassette. Part of *Literature for Children.* Series 1.

Tells how Holling C. Holling created *Pagoo* from idea through research, writing, and illustrating to printing and publishing.

95. Weiss, Ava. "The Artist at Work: The Art Director." *Horn Book* 61, no. 3 (May/June, 1985): 269–279.

Some small b & w illustrations. Describes how she became an art director and details her work on picture books throughout their production.

96. Wilson, Rodger B. "The Genesis of a Picturebook: A Personal Journal of the Creation of a Children's Picturebook from the Conception to Final Printing." M.A. Thesis, Ohio State University, Columbus, 1979. 123pp.

A brief history, with particular attention to the technical means of printing illustrations, sets up a thorough chronological analysis of the varied experiences involved in creating and having a picture book published.

97. Zwicker, Marilyn. "Creating Children's Books at the Rochester Folk Art Guild." *Wilson Library Bulletin* 55, no. 2 (October, 1980): 118–122.

Description of the process used by the guild in designing and processing general picture book titles.

PART III

Criticism of Children's Picture Books, Including Their "Use" with Children

98.   Abrahamson, Richard F., and Robert Stewart. "Movable Books—A New Golden Age." *Language Arts* 59, no. 4 (April, 1982): 342–347.

A discussion of some of the new "toy" or movable books, how they are made, and their authors. Reproductions of old ones are noted.

99.   Alderman, Belle, and Lauren Harman, eds. *The Imagineers: Writing and Illustrating Children's Books.* Canberra, Australia: Reading Time, 1983. 171pp.

Some b & w illustrations and photographs. Collection of papers given at the Children's Book Council of Australia ACT Branch October Seminars 1981–1982. Illustrators discussing their work include: Bruce Treloar, pp. 41–53, on the development of *Bumble's Dream* from gestation to finished book. Pamela Allen, pp. 133–148, tells how she does picture books in general and of some problems with particular books. Elizabeth Honey, pp. 155–168, discusses how she became an illustrator and how she works. Brief biographical sketches and references are included for all. The work of the editor is covered by Kay Ronai, pp. 113–125. Information on judging for the Book of the Year awards is given by Diana Page and Belle Alderman on pp. 69–99.

100. *AIGA Journal*. Volume III, no. 3. "Children's Books."

A series of short articles cover the judging of this America Institute of Graphic Arts exhibition of children's books; problem of designing for the pre-school group; illustrations in school textbooks; designing books for practical uses; and a review of foreign picture books.

101. Apseloff, Marilyn. "Books for Babies: Learning Toys or Pre-Literature." *Children's Literature Association Quarterly* 12, no. 2 (Summer, 1987): 63–66.

Analyzes both text and illustration of some of the many new books for the very young, and questions their educational value, with a mention of the qualities of illustration.

102. Arakelian, Paul G. "Text and Illustration: A Stylistic Analysis of Books by Sendak and Mayer." *Children's Literature Association Quarterly* 10, no. 3 (Fall, 1985): 122–127.

Comparison of Mayer's *There's a Nightmare in My Closet* with Sendak's *Where the Wild Things Are* using page layouts and sentence structures. Combines formal techniques with considerable descriptive information.

   * Bader, Barbara. *American Picture books from Noah's Ark to the Beast Within*. Cited above as item 4.

   * Barr, John. *Illustrated Children's Books*. Cited above as item 5.

103. Barron, Pamela, and Jennifer Q. Burley, eds. *Jump Over the Moon: Selected Professional Readings*. New York: Holt, Rinehart and Winston, 1984. 512pp.

A collection of reading from many sources on the "concerns of the literature for early childhood" expressing many points of view and made to accompany a television course co-produced by the University of South Carolina and the South Carolina Educational Television Network.

Many articles are directly concerned with illustration and picture books and some appear separately listed in this bibliography. Of particular interest are Part 6, "Illustrations," pp. 157–192; and Part 11, "Sharing Picture Books," pp. 348–491.

104. Bator, Robert. *Signposts to Criticism of Children's Literature*. Chicago: A.L.A., 1983. 345pp.

This collection of articles, speeches, etc. on aspects of children's literature includes a section, "Picture books," pp. 149–165. After an introduction, the articles that are included are: Kenneth Marantz, "The Picture Book as Art Object: A Call for Balanced Reviewing," pp. 152–156. Blair Lent, "There's Much More to the Picture Than Meets the Eye," pp. 156–161, including the role of the artist as well as discussion of picture books. Margaret Matthias and Graciela Italiano, "Louder Than a Thousand Words," pp. 161–165, analyzes the importance of illustration and style.

105. Berridge, Celia. "Illustrators, Books, and Children: An Illustrator's Viewpoint." *Children's Literature in Education* 2, no. 1 (Spring, 1980): 21–30.

Review of a range of studies relating to children's responses to pictures indicated inconclusive or erroneous findings. Comments by some major illustrators point out their alienation from any child audience. The question about the conscious creating of illustrations to meet the tastes of children remains a matter of "splendid controversy."

106. Bitzer, Lucy. "The Art of Picture Books: Beautiful Treasures of Bookmaking." *Top of the News* 38, no. 3 (Spring, 1982): 226–232.

The Art Director of Four Winds Press analyzes media, style and expressive content of many historic and contemporary illustrators. Also details what to look for from dust jacket on through end papers, half-titles, etc. An appreciation of the qualities evident in the best. Six small b & w illustrations.

107. Blumenthal, Eileen Polley. "Picture Books For Chinese Children." *Intellect* 106 (March, 1978): 357–358.

With photographs of examples. From her dissertation at the University of Michigan, shows how moral models are reinforced in the children's books which cost little or nothing and are issued in editions of a million.

108. Bosma, Bette. *Fairy Tales, Fables, Legends and Myths: Using Folk Literature in Your Classroom.* New York: Teachers College, 1987. 116pp.

Three pages call attention to the values of illustrations in some books and suggest a few projects for appreciation and making pictures. Although no criteria are given, illustrations "worthy of note" are starred in the extensive list of recommended books.

109. Brown, Marcia. *Lotus Seeds: Children, Pictures and Books.* New York: Scribner's, 1985. 224pp.

Fourteen speeches and other pieces written by Brown in the years from 1949–1984, including her three Caldecott speeches, cover such topics as the world of children's books, her own techniques of work, and her reflections on people, life and art. She writes from the heart of the picture book renaissance, bringing to facts and names a special sense of spirituality.

110. Butler, Francelia, ed. *Children's Literature Volume 1.* Philadelphia: Temple, 1972. 186pp.

Includes Julie Carlson McAlpine, "Sendak Confronts the 'Now' Generation," pp. 138–142, covering Sendak's answers to questions about his work at the University of Connecticut, December 10, 1970.

111. ———. *Children's Literature Volume 2.* Philadelphia: Temple, 1973. 256pp.

Includes Annabelle Simon Cahn's "Leo Lionni, Artist and Philosopher," pp. 123–129, which discusses his life, studio, technique, works and philosophy, including quotations. Two b & w illustrations.

112. ⸻. *Children's Literature Volume 3*. Philadelphia: Temple, 1974. 256pp.

Includes Justin G. Schiller's "Artistic Awareness in Early Children's Books," pp. 175–185, historic notes read at the Second Children's Book Showcase, Drexel, March 19, 1973.

113. ⸻. *Children's Literature Volume 6*. Philadelphia: Temple, 1977. 298pp.

Includes: Christa Kamenetsky's "Arthur Rackham and the Romantic Tradition: The Question of Polarity and Ambiguity," pp. 115–129, with b & w illustrations; Jennifer R. Waller's "Maurice Sendak and the Blakean Vision of Childhood," pp. 130–141; reviews of Newbery and Caldecott winners 1975–76 by David L. Greene, pp 191–194.

114. ⸻. *Children's Literature Volume 12*. New Haven: Yale University, 1984. 255pp.

Includes Geraldine DeLuca's "Exploring the Levels of Childhood: The Allegorical Sensibility of Maurice Sendak," pp. 3–24, with some discussion of the visual aspects of his work.

115. ⸻. *Children's Literature Volume 13*. New Haven: Yale University, 1985. 228pp.

Includes Ruth B. Bottligheimer's "Iconographic Continuity in Illustrations of *The Goosegirl*," pp. 49–71, which analyzes many versions in the history of the tale; Michael Steig's "Reading *Outside Over There*," pp. 139–153, analyzes several reviews of the book and gives Steig's own interpretation including the illustrations.

116. Callahan, Joan F. "The Picturebook as the Central Focus of an Elementary Art Curriculum." M.A. Thesis, Ohio State University, Columbus. 149pp.

Using Bruner's "spiral curriculum" model as a jumping off point, this study makes a case for picture books as esthetic objects which can help children learn about the structure of art history as well as the methods of the professional artist to develop critical and appreciative skills needed in all esthetic enterprises.

117. Chambers, Nancy, ed. *The Signal Approach to Children's Books.* Metuchen, N.J.: Scarecrow, 1980. 352pp.

Some b & w illustrations. Selections from the publication *Signal* include: "Signal quote" from Edward Ardizzone, pp. 32–33, an analysis of what the good illustrator does and what skills are needed. "Picture books and verse," pp. 64–65, lists important contemporary British author-illustrators. "The Cinderella story 1724–1919," by Irene Whalley on p. 144, describes early illustrations.

118. Chapman, Diane L. *The New Look of Children's Picture Books.* ERIC Microfiche ED 189607 80. 29pp.

Paper presented at the annual meeting of the International Reading Association in St. Louis, May, 1980. Summarizes innovations of style and media used, lists some artists and styles, and how media used reflect character. Discusses photography, wordless books, "problem books" and gives lists of some of these and some evaluation.

119. "Children's Book Illustrators Play Favorites." *Wilson Library Bulletin* 52, no. 2 (October, 1977): 165–173.

Arnold Lobel, Karla Kuskin, Trina Hyman and Tomie de Paola talk about their favorite illustrators and why they like them.

120. *Children's Books International 1.* Boston: Boston Public Library, 1976. 134pp.

The proceedings of a conference include an interview with a Japanese artist (Kazue Mizumura); an illustrated talk on illustrators of Grimm tales; and a panel discussing some issues of illustrating in "The Business of Books." 60 pages are devoted to a catalog of titles exhibited. There are no illustrations of books reproduced.

121. *Children's Books International 2.* Boston: Boston Public Library, 1977. 154pp.

The proceedings of a conference include an illustrated talk mainly about the animated books of Meggendorfer (late 19th century); a history of the Biennale of Illustrators in Bratislava; and a catalog (65pp.) of displayed books. No reproductions included.

122. Cianciolo, Patricia. "Developing the Beginning Reading Process with Picture Books." Paper presented at the Meeting of the "Five Year Olds in School" Conference, East Lansing, January 9–10, 1987. ERIC Document ED 280013. 26pp.

Research, especially in the 1970's, has shown the importance of picture books, especially those of quality, to a child's early reading process. Of five qualities listed by the author, #3: Relation of text and illustration, and #4: Illustration quality beyond the literal, pp. 2–3, are of special interest. Includes analysis of some picture books and a fine professional bibliography.

123. ———. *Illustrations in Children's Books.* 2nd ed. Dubuque: Wm. C. Brown, 1976. 210pp. (Literature for Children series.)

Some b & w illustrations. Designed mainly for teachers, but also librarians and parents should also learn from the large quantities of information provided. Chapters describe how to appraise illustrations; identify styles (taken from the art world) which she feels illustrated books have in common; explain many of the media and techniques illustrators use; and finally offer a variety of means for the illustrations to be used in schools. Half the book is devoted to an annotated bibliography of illustrated books, list of some wordless books, and basic information about Caldecott titles and those from the Children's Book Showcase.

124. _____. *Picture Books for Children.* 2nd ed., rev. and enlarged. Chicago: American Library Association, 1981. 237pp.

Some b & w illustrations. Introduction, pp. 1–29, discusses what a picture book is, her criteria for selections, some notes on styles of art and in picture books, and categories of response and subjects. The remaining pages are an annotated bibliography arranged in categories from "Me and my family," out to others, the world and imaginary worlds. Index of authors, illustrators and titles.

125. _____. "Use Wordless Picture Books to Teach Reading, Visual Literacy and to Study Literature." *Top of the News* 29 (April, 1973): 226–234.

Along with analysis of the literary devices and elements in these books there is some analysis of style, also bibliography of useful books. Also in Mary Lou White's, *Children's Literature.*

126. Cott, Jonathan. *Pipers at the Gates of Dawn: The Wisdom of Children's Literature.* New York: Random House, 1983. 327pp.

Some b & w illustrations and photographs. Introduction has personal reflections on the importance of children's literature. "The Good Dr. Seuss," pp. 3–37, visit, interview and critical discussion, including two-page history of first children's book. "Maurice Sendak, King of All Wild Things," pp. 41–84, includes biographical information, criticism and commentary. "William Steig and his path," pp. 88–133, includes an interview, an analysis of early cartoons and detailed discussion of books.

*   _____, ed. *Masterworks of Children's Literature, Volume Seven: Victorian Color Picture Books.* Cited above as item 16.

127. Crago, Maureen, and Hugh Crago. *Prelude to Literacy: A Preschool Child's Encounter with Picture and Story.* Carbondale: Southern Illinois University, 1983. 294pp.

Reports on but also attempts to interpret one child's comments on color and other aspects of pictures in books from age 12 months to five years. Art examples from "fine art" are included. Discusses picture preference in light of previous research.

128. Cross, Jennifer Lynn. "Artistic Interpretation in the Fairytale Picturebook." M.A. Thesis, Ohio State University, Columbus, 1987. 234pp.

First establishing the symbolism and form of traditional Western fairy tales, the study investigates the problems of illustration within this tradition by means of analysis of several versions of Grimm's tales and through creating an original picture book.

129. Cullinan, Bernice E., ed. *Children's Literature in the Reading Program.* Newark, Delaware: International Reading Association, 1987. 171pp.

Chapter 8, "Enriching the Arts and Humanities through Children's Books," by Sam Leaton Sebesta on pp. 77–81 briefly is concerned with artists of both "fine art" and picture books and discusses ways to introduce and discuss their work with children.

130. _____, with Mary K. Karrer, and Arlene M. Pillar. *Literature and the Child.* New York: Harcourt Brace Jovanovich, 1981. 594pp.

Includes some photographs and some color illustrations. Basically a textbook for Children's Literature classes. Includes "Historical View of Children and Books," pp. 35–69. Chapter on picture book is by subject, with a few pages on art techniques, and on criteria for selection. Profiles of book authors and illustrators with quotations and critical analyses are throughout the book. Useful teaching suggestions and appendices.

131. Darling, Harold, and Peter Neumeyer, eds. *Image and Maker: An Annual Dedicated to the Consideration of Book Illustration.* La Jolla, California: Green Tiger, 1984. 56pp.

Profusely illustrated in b & w with tipped-in color plates. Contents include:
"How Picture Books Work," by Perry Nodelman, pp. 1–12, tries to show "how very much pictures control our responses to words" by analyzing some examples.
"What Manner of Beast? Illustrations of *Beauty and the Beast*," by Stephen Canham, pp. 13–25, compares several versions and their effect.
"Luther Daniels Bradley: Guide to the Great Somewhere-or-Other," by Helen Borgens, pp. 26–36, is an appreciation of Bradley's life and work.
"Jessie Willcox Smith," by Carolyn Haywood, pp. 37–42, covers Smith's life and work.
"The Great Catalogs: An Alternate Way to Study Early Children's Book Illustration," by Kenneth E. Luther, pp. 43–54, describes catalogs from several sources and gives order information.

132. Darton, Frederick Joseph Harvey. *Modern Book Illustration in Great Britain and America.* London/New York: The Studio Limited/William Edwin Rudge, 1931. (Special Winter number of "The Studio," edited by C. Geoffrey Holme.) 144pp.

Almost every other page a full-page b & w illustration up to p. 79, seven in color. Pages 80–144 all illustrations. What is "illustration"? Some discussion of the history of technique, mainly in adult books, with children's, on p. 75.

133. de Paola, Tomie. "From Lascaux to Hi-Tech." Fourth Annual Naomi Chase Lecture. *New Books for Young Readers* (June 2, 1983): Minneapolis: University of Minnesota, 1984. Pp. 18–23.

A personal view of the role of the artist-illustrator through history.

134. Dondis, Donis A. *A Primer of Visual Literacy.* Cambridge: Massachusetts Institute of Technology, 1973. 194pp.

Useful for acquiring vocabulary for approaching and analyzing two-dimensional graphic imagery. Chapter VI, pp. 104–127, uses simple contrasts to point out techniques used by designers; e.g., transparency vs. opacity.

135. Dooley, Patricia. "The Window in the Book: Conventions in the Illustration of Children's Books." *Wilson Library Bulletin* 55, no. 2 (October, 1980): 108–112.

Some history of the appearance of illustrations and their points of view, and how technology has led to some changes.

136. Dorfman, Ariel. *The Empire's Old Clothes: What the Lone Ranger, Babar, and Other Innocent Heroes Do to Our Minds.* New York: Pantheon, 1983. 225pp.

Nothing on illustration, but a fascinating socio-political analysis of Babar, among others.

137. Dressel, Janice Hartwick. "Abstraction in Illustration: Is It Appropriate for Children?" *Children's Literature in Education.* Volume 15, no. 2 (Summer, 1984): 103–112.

An argument that first sketches the 20th-century evolution of "abstract" art and then makes a case for its suitability for picture book illustration. "Abstract art must be interpreted on the basis of its existence alone. . . ."

138. Driesson, Diane Z. "A Description of a Select Group of Six Fifth Grade Students' Response to Picturebooks." Ph.D. Dissertation, Ohio State University, Columbus, 1984. 190pp.

How do children with several years of picture-book school experience respond to picture books in terms of preferences and varying attributes of book design? An open-ended questioning procedure is used in small group and individual settings.

139. Durand, Marion, et Gerard Bertrand. *L'Image dans le Livre pour Enfants*. Paris: L'Ecole des Loisirs, 1975. 220pp.

Profusely illustrated in color and b & w with examples from many countries. This comprehensive treatment of children's book illustration deserves the wide readership only a translation into english could deliver. The analysis of style, the discussion of the role of word and text and their interrelationship, the treatment of the principle characters, human or animal, realistic or caricature, serious or humorous, are all done with a keen analytic eye and many examples. The discussion of the variety of contemporary styles, including photography, is of particular interest. Political and social connotations are also covered.

140. _____. "One Hundred Years of Illustrations in French Children's Books." (Translated by Diana Wormuth.) *Yale French Studies*, no. 43 (1969): 85–96.

Demonstration of the claim that children's book illustration has suffered "a gradual impoverishment" by critical analysis of several exemplars. Speculation that the low status of illustrators today compared with 100 years ago may be a major cause of the decline.

141. Duvoisin, Roger. "Children's Book Illustration: The Pleasures and the Problems." *Top of the News* (November, 1965): 299–316.

His views on "what is an illustration and what makes it beautiful" from an "artistic point of view." He discusses the design problems involved and how they relate to the audience of children, the role of abstraction, some history of illustration and its relation to art history and painting.

142. Egoff, Sheila A., ed. *One Ocean Touching: Papers from the First Pacific Rim Conference on Children's Literature*. New York: Scarecrow, 1979. 252pp.

Includes: Margaret Johnston, "Surprised by Joy: The World of Picture-Books," pp. 147–154. Picture books as "...basis of all literature, so also...the basis of art criticism." Discusses briefly what makes a good picture book, and mentions some books that she feels have the important qualities from the U.S., England, and Canada.

Graham Booth, "The Price of Being an Artist," pp. 155–163. How he became a book illustrator; the reality of working as an illustrator; his problems and fears; his working methods and the economics of the business.

Elizabeth Cleaver, "Picture Books as Artform," pp. 195–196. She discusses the influences on her work; her personal feelings and method of working; the economic hardship of the business.

143. _____. *The Republic of Childhood: A Critical Guide to Canadian Children's Literature in English.* 2nd ed. Toronto: Oxford University Press, 1975. 335pp.

Chapter 9, "Illustration and design," pp. 255–270, covers some Canadian illustrators of the past plus newer illustrators and their techniques.
Chapter 10, pp. 271–291, "Picture-books and picture storybooks," discusses these as a more recent and independent development from illustration alone: "a separate genre," distinguishes between picture books and picture storybooks and gives many examples of current books and their creators in Canada.
Lists of titles and award winners for illustration included.

144. Eisner, Elliot W., ed. *Reading, the Arts, and the Creation of Meaning.* Washington, D.C.: National Art Education Association, 1978. 160pp.

Includes Kenneth Marantz, "On the Mysteries of Reading and Art: The Picture-book as Art Object," pp. 71–87, which investigates some of the problems that differentiate written language and picture as symbol systems. Denies the reasonability of art as a language and points out that the reading process is still a mysterious one because there are no "global equivalents of word signs."

145. Elleman, Barbara. "Caldecott Winners are Picture Perfect."
      Gifted Children Monthly 7, no. 6 (June, 1986): 16–17, 20.

      Summarizes Caldecott Medal background and analyzes current
      winners and some of the best from the past.

146. _____. "Discovering Art Through Picture Books." *Gifted
      Children Newsletter* 4, no. 12 (December, 1983): 16–17.

      Giving many examples of picture books to use, Elleman shows
      how to introduce the art to children.

147. *Enjoying Illustrations.* (Sound Filmstrip.) Verdugo City,
      California: Pied Piper, 1971. 1 Filmstrip, 1 cassette. Part of
      Literature for Children Series 3.

      Covers 40 artists. Discusses the role of the illustrations and
      encourages comparisons of versions of the same story.

148. Eyre, Frank. *British Children's Books in the Twentieth Century.*
      New York: E.P. Dutton, 1971. 153pp.

      "Books with pictures," discusses what illustration should be and
      what makes a successful picture book. Also gives history of
      picture books in Britain and mentions many books both familiar
      and unfamiliar to Americans. His appendix on books from
      Commonwealth countries mentions some regional picture books,
      authors and illustrators. "Award Winners" includes those from
      Britain, Australia, New Zealand and Canada.

149. Fox, Geoff, and Graham Hammond, eds. *Responses to
      Children's Literature: Proceedings of the Fourth Symposium of
      the International Research Society for Children's Literature Held
      at the University of Exeter, September 9–12, 1978.* New York:
      K.G. Saur, 1980. 141pp.

      Includes Stuart Amor, "A Functional Approach to Illustrations
      in Children's Books—The Work of Frantisek Holesovsky,"

pp. 76–80, summarizes the approach of the Czech theorist as a possible spur to analysis or further research.

Agnia Barto, "Children's Responses to Illustrations of Poetry," pp. 81–87, contains personal experiences and reflections on these responses.

Carmen Bravo-Villasante, "Text and Illustration in Emblem Books," pp. 88–91, contains historical information on these symbolic images.

Patricia Cianciolo, "Children's Responses to Illustrations in Picture Books," pp. 102–108, summarizes studies of responses and references and relates them to children's previous experience.

Janine Despinette, "Modern Picture Books and the Child's Visual Sense," pp. 109–116, discusses the importance of the illustration beyond simply the didactic, and the psychological and aesthetic effects of the picture on the child, giving some examples from specific books.

Joseph Schwarcz, "The Continuous Narrative Technique in Children's Literature," pp. 117–126, gives an analysis of illustration of time passing and research on its psychological effect on children of different ages.

Bela Toth, "Psychological Relationships Between Text and Illustration," pp. 129–130, describes experiments on 8–10-year-olds' reactions to the interaction of text and picture, and the effect of the illustration.

150. Freeman, Graydon La Verne, and Ruth Sunderlin Freeman. *The Child and His Picture Book.* Watkins Glen, New York: Century House, 1933. Updated 1967. 111pp.

Illustrations in b & w. Original nine chapters discuss "function" of picture books, some existing books of the time, adult opinion of picture books and the choices children make of picture books and their illustrations.

The updated section rechecks some of the data from the earlier study. Appendix lists facts on some illustrators.

151. Gainer, Ruth Strays. "Beyond Illustration: Information About Art in Children's Picture Books." *Art Education* (March, 1982): 116–119.

How to use picture books to show a variety of ways artists deal with problems to help children in art classes solve theirs. Values in using these books are delineated. Includes a list of particularly rich sources.

* Georgiou, Constantine. *Children and Their Literature*. Cited above as item 25.

152. Giff, Patricia Reilly; Martha Belden; and Mary Jane Mangini Rossi. "Look Again: Picture Books Are More Than Pictures." *Instructor* (September, 1985): 56–62.

Analysis of picture books with special qualities of format, story or added meaning for use with students.

153. Gill, Bob, and John Lewis. *Illustration: Aspects and Directions*. New York: Reinhold, 1964. 96pp.

General discussion of the qualities all illustration should possess. A dozen pages devoted to "children's books" provide a jet plane's-eye-view of the history and an equally brief but barbed critique of the current scene. More illustrations than text in b & w and color.

154. Goldsmith, Evelyn. *Research into Illustration: An Approach and Review*. Cambridge, England: Cambridge University Press, 1984. 487pp.

A valuable compilation and analysis of current (mainly post-1970) research studies "applicable to educational illustration in general," gleaned from visual communication, psychology and education. Sections include: "Use of Illustration," pp. 9–120; "Analysis of Illustration" (the major section), pp. 121–390; and "Research into Illustration," pp. 391–424. Focus is on the pragmatics of communicating information rather than the esthetics of pictures. Excellent use is made of 205 b & w illustrations and over 200 studies.

155. _____, ed. *Research into Illustration 2*. Proceedings of the Conference Held on 16/17 February, 1984 in the Sallis Benney

Theatre, Faculty of Art and Design, Brighton Polytechnic, Grand Parade, Brighton. Brighton, Eng.: Brighton Polytechnic, 1984. 153pp.

The general question raised was "Do illustrations for children need specific considerations . . . ?" Are they different? Includes "Some Research Findings" by Evelyn Goldsmith, pp. 3–11, her concerns about how children perceive the illustrations, in part or as a whole, alone or in sequence. "Deceptive Beetles" by Tony Potter, pp. 13–28, discusses how children perceive pictures at various ages and differences between illustrations for picture books and those for informational books. "Hang the Children—What About the Books?" by Brian Alderson, pp. 29–35, analyzes Errol LeCain's version of the Snow Queen to show the importance Alderson places on the relation of illustration to text, and also raises concerns about the paucity and difficulty of research about picture book illustration. "Child as Parent to the Illustrator: Drawing and Painting with Words," by John Vernon Lord, pp. 37–108, analyzes in detail how many illustrators work, with concerns of text and picture composition regardless of the age of the child consumer. Summary of "Illustration from a Publisher's Point of View," by Tom Maschler, p. 104. "Books, Illustrations and Child Development; How Much Are We Ever Likely to Know?," by Nicholas Tucker, pp. 111–119, covering areas of research in how children perceive illustrations and how limited we are in what we can find out. "How Does Perception Develop?," by Richard Gregory, pp. 121–122. "A Very Brief Talk...?," by Raymond Briggs, pp. 123–132, which is a personal account of his feelings about his life as author–illustrator, in the style of his books, with some letters to and from children. Reports from leaders of discussion groups on the main subject and chair's summary, pp. 133–148. Some b & w illustrations. List of delegates attending appended.

156. "Graphic Gallery." *The Horn Book* 62 (November–December, 1986): 695–723.

A jury of Richard Bartlett, David Macaulay and Ed Young chooses fourteen picture books (1980–1984) and presents them with their "observations about the visual aspects of the genre."

Graphis magazine. "International Journal of Graphic Art and Applied Art" (Zurich: Walter Herdag, The Graphis Press) has occasional issues on "children's book illustration" (some have also been issued as separate expanded volumes numbered 1, 2, 3 and 4) covering the international world of children's book illustration. Some of these are described here. All are profusely illustrated in both b & w and color.

157. *Graphis* 23, no. 131 (1967): 206–315.

Includes: Arsen Pohribny, "New Trends in Czechoslovak Children's Books," pp. 208–215, 310, which describes a new artistic freedom and analyzes some winners at the Bologna Book Fair.

Robert F. Klein, "Children's Books in France," pp. 216–223, 304 mainly gives examples; Hans A. Halbey, "The German Picture-Book Gains Ground," pp. 224–231, 306 discusses some illustrators, German and not, and credits modern art with opening children to less traditional illustration.

Judy Taylor and John Ryder, "Children's Book Illustration in England," pp. 232–241, 306 covers a rising new wave of British illustrators to challenge U.S. domination.

Bettina Hurlimann, "Notes on Japanese Picturebooks," pp. 242–249, 304, discusses artists and typical qualities.

Olga Siemaszkova, "Thoughts on Children's Books in Poland," pp. 250–261, 304, covers the current rapid development and booming business, and suggests that they may prepare children for the adult world while educating parent's tastes.

Bettina Hurlimann, "The Swiss Picture-Book Today," pp. 262–271, 307, covers current producers.

Harlan Quist, "Children's Book Production in the U.S.A.," pp. 272–295, 312–313, covers the current "boom" but is concerned with the quality of what is published.

158. *Graphis* 27, no. 155 (1971–1972).

Contains articles by Franz Casper on the "Children's Picture Books Today," pp. 301–303 in Italy; pp. 306–312 in Scandinavia; pp. 296–297 in Russia; pp. 298–300 in Hungary; pp. 304–305 in Austria; also includes: Horst Kunnemann, "Present and Future Evolution of the German Picture-Book," pp. 228–241; Bettina Hurlimann, "Notes on Japanese Picturebooks," pp. 268–273, which updates her last report. Zbigniew Rychlick, "Children's Book Illustration in Poland," pp. 274–283, with examples.

159. *Graphis* 31, no. 177 (July, 1975), also called "Third International Survey of Children's Book Illustration." 136pp.

Includes a special introduction by Virginia Haviland and the following articles:

Bettina Hurlimann, "German Picture-Books of the 19th Century," pp. 2–11 (not in magazine), an illustrated survey.

Jerome Snyder, "U.S. Children's Books in a Changing World," pp. 12–28, covers the effects of the unsettled society with examples.

John Ryder, "Children's Book Illustration in Britain," pp. 30–37, feels there is little new except from Australia but shows more from old favorites.

Christine Chagnoux, "New Children's Books—Or Parents' Books?—in France," pp. 38–47, feels children have not been consulted enough, and that Babar is "still king."

Ingeborg Ramseger, "New Trends in Children's Books in Germany," pp. 48–59, feels 1969 was a turning point when facts and realism as well as beauty were demanded for all classes of children, but quality was not to be sacrificed. New names noted.

Jurg Schatzmann, "Tradition and Internationalism in the Swiss Children's Book," pp. 60–75, covers both co-productions and purely Swiss artists, old and new with examples.

Tadashi Matsui, "The Japanese Picture-Book in Past and Present," pp. 76–83, gives a brief history, some Western influences, and examples of current works.

Mieczyslaw Piotrowski, "Polish Illustrators and the Children's Book," pp. 84–93, covers current continuation of high standards.

Dusan Roll, "Contemporary Children's Book Illustration in Czechoslovakia," pp. 94–99, discusses high standards set by the art school of Bratislava and the many artists doing book illustration.

Anna Katharina Ulrich, "The Future Evolution of the Art of the Picture-Book," pp. 100–115, raises questions about the handsome expensive picture book with "sketchy content" in a future of reduced publishing and co-publishing and whether any but established authors will find publishers.

Walter Abegg, "ABC and Counting Books," pp. 116–123 (not in magazine), gives brief survey. Short biographies of illustrators are included in book only.

160. *Graphis* 34, no. 200 (April, 1979), also called "Fourth International Survey of Children's Book Illustration." Edited by Walter Herdeg. Pp. 468–615.

Includes notes on 1979 as the Year of the Child by Hans Conzett and "The Rights of the Child." Also:

Michael Patrick Hearn, "Ivan Y. Bilibin; The Leading Illustrator of Children's Books in Pre-Revolutionary Russia," pp. 472–481 (not in magazine), a brief summary with many examples; "Current Picture-Book Publishing in the United States of America," pp. 482–501, covers lower sales and the revival of interest in fantasy and fairy tale.

Brian Alderson, "Children's Books in Britain: Divergent Styles and Occupational Highlights," pp. 502–515, discusses the very wide range and the importance of the whole rather than individual pictures.

Christine Chagnoux, "French Children's Books: Cult of the New v. the Old Favorites," pp. 516–525, discusses what is popular, notes higher quality of paper and color production.

Hildegard Krahe, "German Picture-Books—A Ray of Hope for Children in an Unkind Age?," pp. 526–541, reflects the continuing production of some artists, the lack of new experimenters, but some rise in fantasy and the fun of toy books.

Bettina Hurlimann, "The International Palette of Swiss Children's Books," pp. 542–559, lists current names.

Tadasi Matsui, "Children's Books in Japan: Rapid Growth and a Promising Future," pp. 560–565, covers this growth.

Danuta Wroblewka, "Children's Book Illustration in Poland: A Landscape with a Rainbow," pp. 566–575, relates illustration to the fine arts in Poland, and notes the young artists' use of color. Dusan Roll, "Children's Books in Czechoslovakia: A Younger Generation Takes Over," pp. 576–583, gives examples of both the old and new artists. Anna Katharina Ulrich, "Notes on the International Picture-Book Scene," pp. 584–599, sees trends of growth and internationalization along with the rise of new themes plus a nostalgia for old favorites. Short biographies of illustrators are in the book but not the magazine.

161. Groff, P. "Should Picture Books and Children Be Matched?" *Language Arts* 54 (1977): 411–417.

Summarizes the previous research on children's preferences and the questions raised. Notes weaknesses. Gives valid reasons for not catering to these preferences but rather for simply selecting quality books. Useful bibliography.

162. Hearne, Betsy. *Choosing Books for Children: A Commonsense Guide*. New York: Delacorte, 1981. 150pp.

Of particular relevance is Chapter IV, pp. 29–49, "The Picture Book for Younger Children—Dead or Alive?," which gives criteria for judging and some examples of successful books.

163. _____, and Marilyn Kaye, eds. *Celebrating Children's Books*. New York: Lothrop, Lee and Shepard, 1981. 244pp.

The articles in this collection that concern picture books are: Arnold Lobel, "A Good Picture Book Should...," pp. 73–80, gives his criteria for a successful picture book, and describes his motivations. David Macaulay, "How to Create a Successful Nonfiction Picture Book," pp. 97–101, is a humorous discussion of all the wrong "rules."

164. Heins, Ethel. "Storytelling Through Art: Pretense or Performance?" *Horn Book* 59 (February, 1983): 14–15.

Raises questions of "artistic quality" and which illustrators possess it.

* Huck, Charlotte S., with Susan Hepler and Janet Hickman. *Children's Literature in the Elementary School.* Cited above as item 30.

165. *Human—and Anti-Human—Values in Children's Books.* New York: Council on Interracial Books for Children, 1976. 279pp.

A completely different way of looking at the illustrations in picture books. Check lists rate both "art" and "words" on racist, sexist, materialist, individualist, ageist, conformist and escapist grounds, and then rate "literary quality" and "art quality" of selected books, "pre-school and early years," pp. 27–84. Illustrators included are indexed.

166. Hurlimann, Bettina. *Picture-Book World.* London: Oxford, and Cleveland: World, 1968. 216pp.

An international survey, country by country, stressing the art. An "anthology of reproductions" in b & w and color fill a good part of the book.

167. *The Illustrator as Storyteller: Caldecott Medal and Honor Books 1938–1984.* Catalog of an exhibition drawn largely from the Kerlan Collection and organized with University Art Museum in conjunction with "The Illustrator as Storyteller," a Conference held at the University of Chicago and Chicago Public Library, October 19–20, 1984. Minneapolis: University of Minnesota, 1984. 20pp.

On pp. 3–5 Ellin Greene gives some historical background on picture books and on the Caldecott Medal. Brief introductions to each type of book illustration shown followed by details about the illustration and one b & w example for each.

* *Images a la Page: Une Histoire de l'Image dans les Livres pour l'Enfants.* Cited above as item 33.

* Jones, Linda Harris. *A Comparison of the Works of Walter Crane, Randolph Caldecott and Kate Greenaway and Their Contributions to Children's Literature.* Cited above as item 36.

168. Katz, Elia. *Children's Preferences for Traditional and Modern Paintings.* New York: Columbia University Press, 1944. 101pp.

In this study of historic interest children preferred "traditional" rather than "modern" art. The children are sorted by grade level, sex and socio-economic level.

169. Kiefer, Barbara. "The Artist, the Book and the Child." Paper delivered at the "Artist as Storyteller" Symposium in Chicago, October 19–20, 1984. ERIC Document ED 253868. 30pp.

Defines the elements of design used by the artist in picture books as well as paintings to convey expressive contents. Notes on how children responded to these qualities in observed classroom settings.

170. _____. "The Child and the Picture Book: Create Live Circuits." *Children's Literature Association Quarterly* 2, no. 2, (Summer, 1986): 63–68.

Report of a study done in elementary classrooms observing and talking with children about their responses to a variety of picture books. She found that responses over a period of months became increasingly complex and independent of third party intervention.

171. _____. "Looking Beyond Picture Book Preferences." *Horn Book* 61, no. 6 (November–December, 1985): 705–713.

Details a study done with seven- and eight-year-olds using several complex and demanding picture books to show that given an environment that fosters inquiry and encourages introspection, young children do respond profoundly to the esthetic qualities of the books.

172. _____. "The Response of Children in a Combination First/
     Second Grade Classroom to Picture Books in a Variety of
     Artistic Styles." *Journal of Research and Development in
     Education* 16, no. 3 (Spring, 1983): 14–20.

     Report of observations over a ten-week period shows variations,
     and indicates the importance of where the books are placed, the
     teachers, and of the illustration's position in the book as a whole.
     Changes over time as well as differences among students are
     noted.

173. _____. "The Response of Primary Children to Picturebooks."
     Ph.D. Dissertation, Ohio State University, Columbus, 1982.
     268pp.

     An ethnographic study of first and second graders over a three
     month period demonstrated the significance of extended periods of
     time needed for children to appreciate picture books and pointed
     out the weaknesses of most preference studies which deal with
     excerpted illustrations in a very short time-span.

174. Kiefer, Monica Mary. *American Children Through Their Books,
     1700–1835.* Philadelphia: University of Pennsylvania, 1948.
     248pp.

     Some b & w reproductions from early books. Although only pp.
     6–11 deal with the illustrations, the book fills in background
     information on children and their lives at the time.

175. Kingman, Lee; Joanna Foster; and Ruth Giles Lontoft,
     compilers. *Illustrators of Children's Books, 1957–1966.*
     Boston: Horn Book, 1968. 295pp.

     Many b & w illustrations and one color spread example. Part I,
     "A Decade of Illustration in Children's Books," includes:
     "One Wonders" by Marcia Brown, pp. 2–27, analyzes the current
     flood of picture books with perceptive comments on some artists
     and their work.

"Color Separation" by Adrienne Adams, pp. 28–35, analyzes the process in detail.
"The Artist and His Editor" by Grace Allen Hogarth, pp. 36–53, discusses many illustrators, their relationship with their editors and their texts, and the effects of new technology.
"Beatrix Potter: Centenary of an Artist-Writer" by Rumer Godden, pp. 54–64, treats her life and work.
Part II, "Biographies," pp. 66–197, and Part III, "Bibliographies," pp. 200–287, are like earlier editions. See Bertha E. Mahony and Bertha Mahony Miller for earlier volumes in this series.

176. ———; Grace Allen Hogarth; and Harriet Quimby, compilers. *Illustrators of Children's Books, 1967–1976*. Boston: Horn Book, 1978. 290pp.

Many b & w and some color illustrations. Part I, "A Decade of Illustration in Children's Books," includes:
"Book Illustration: The State of the Art" by Walter Lorraine, pp. 2–19, an in-depth analysis of the works of some of the illustrators active in what he calls "a period of renaissance," and whether their art also tells a story.
"A View From the Island: European Picture Books 1967–1976" by Brian Alderson, pp. 20–43, discusses the important books and trends in criticism he sees.
"Where the Old Meets the New: The Japanese Picture Book" by Teiji Seta and Momoko Ishii, pp. 44–57, a brief summary of the history plus the names and description of the works of the important illustrators active between 1967 and 1976.
"In the Beginning Was the Word...The Illustrated Book 1967–1976" by Treld Pelkey Bicknell, pp. 58–80, analyzes some illustrators as their work relates to the text illustrated in realistic books fiction and non-fiction, in illustrated books rather than picture books.
Part II, "Biographies," pp. 90–171, and Part III, "Bibliographies," pp. 174–254, are like these sections in earlier editions, but do not repeat from the earlier entries, which are listed in a cumulative index.
"Appendix" lists bibliographies for articles in Part I.

177.   Klemin, Diana. *The Art of Art for Children's Books*. New
       York: Potter, 1966. 128pp.

       Identification of about 50 artists whose work exemplifies the
       best in book illustration. They are categorized as Storytellers,
       Poetic and Personal, Imaginary, Collage and Abstraction, and
       Specialist. Each has a b & w or color reproduction accompanied
       by a caption comment by Klemin.

178.   _____. *The Illustrated Book*. New York: Potter, 1970. 159pp.

       Seventy "fine" artists (very few represented by illustrations for
       children's books) are highlighted. Each has an illustration
       reproduced with a half page or so of comment by Klemin.
       Eighteen pages offer limited advice to would-be illustrators.

179.   Kuskin, Karla. "How to Make a Picture Book." *New York
       Times Book Review* (September 24, 1987): 23.

       On problems of matching author and illustrator. Examples of
       historic successful "marriages" and short quotations from several
       illustrators.

180.   Lacy, Lyn E. *Art and Design in Children's Picture Books: An
       Analysis of Caldecott Award-Winning Illustration*. Chicago:
       American Library Association, 1986. 229pp.

       A strong case is made for the study of picture books as a
       significant part of all art appreciation objectives but especially for
       the young child. Most of the extensive analysis of 15 American
       illustrators involves Line, Color, Light and Dark, Shape, and
       Space. But some background material is also provided; and each of
       the sections has many suggestions for further study which include
       related production activities. A glossary but no illustrations
       (readers are requested to obtain the books discussed).
       Illustrators analyzed in detail: The Dillons, Virginia Lee Burton,
       Ed Emberly, Elmer Hader, Ezra Jack Keats, Robert McCloskey,
       Blair Lent, The Petershams, Uri Shvlevitz, Maurice Sendak,
       Roger Duvoisin, and Chris Van Allsburg.

181. Lanes, Selma. *Down the Rabbit Hole: Adventures and Misadventures in the Realm of Children's Literature.* New York: Atheneum, 1971. 239pp.

A major work of analysis and criticism of the picture book. Chapters on the massive increase in numbers since 1945 and on individual "greats" including Sendak and Seuss. Insightful comments on Potter, Rackham, Emberly, Lionni and many more.

182. Larrick, Nancy. "The Changing Picture of Poetry Books for Children." *Wilson Library Bulletin* 55, no. 2 (October, 1980): 113–117.

Sketches descriptive history of illustrated books of poetry from Blake's *Songs of Innocence* to modern collections with photographs.

183. Laughlin, Mildred. "Visual Literacy Through Picture Books K–12: A Curriculum Approach." ERIC Microfiche ED 198814 80. 22pp.

Paper presented at the American Association of School Librarians Conference in Louisville, September 26, 1980. Discusses using picture books to help students "see." David Macaulay's books are considered. Other illustrators mentioned include de Paola, Quackenbush, Anno, Cooney, Hyman, the D'Aulaires and Dillons.

184. Lemieux, Louise. *Pleins Feux Sur la Litterature de Jeunesse au Canada Français.* Montreal: Lemeac, 1972. 337pp.

Lists the limited sources of information on French Canadian children's literature. Chapter V, "Illustration," pp. 107–114, gives further sources in French and other sources for discussion of the art of the picture book. The names of French Canadian illustrators and their own works plus the other texts they have illustrated are given. There is also some discussion of children doing their own illustrations, of cost analysis of book production, some conclusions and recommendations.

185. Lent, Blair. "There's Much More to the Picture Than Meets the Eye." *Wilson Library Bulletin* 52, no. 2 (October, 1977): 161–164.

His analysis of what a picture book is and how the writers and artists work.

186. Lewis, Claudia. "Searching for the Master Touch in Picture Books." *Children's Literature in Education* 15, no. 4 (Winter, 1984): 198–203.

Tries to make a case for some content in picture books being outside the immediate knowledge field of the young child.

*   Lewis, John. *The Twentieth Century Book*. Cited above as item 37.

187. Lewis, Marjorie. "Back to Basics: Reevaluating Picture Books." *School Library Journal* 22, no. 7 (March, 1976): 82–83.

Criticism of "art experimentation" in newer picture books as opposed to the value of the "total experience of story and illustration."

188. *The Lion and the Unicorn: A Critical Journal of Children's Literature.* Special Double Issue, 7/8 (1983–1984) Picture Books. 193pp.

Many b & w illustrations. Includes: Suzanne Rahn, "Beneath the Surface with *Fungus the Bogeyman*," pp. 5–19, places the work with others by Briggs for some analysis of art but mainly of content.
Stephen Roxburgh, "A Picture Equals How Many Words?: Narrative Theory and Picture Books for Children," pp. 20–33, discusses in particular the narrative in Sendak's *Outside Over There*, words and pictures, to show how current critical theory is inadequate to use for discussing the role of the illustrations in the narrative.

Leonard S. Marcus, "The Artist's Other Eye: The Picture Books of Mitsumasa Anno," pp. 34–46, discusses the art of many of his books in detail.

Leonard S. Marcus, "Invention and Discoveries: An Interview with Ann K. Beneduce," pp. 47–63, in which the editor-in-chief of Philomel Books talks about her work, the international world of children's books, and her authors Anno and Carle.

David Pritchard, "'Daddy, Talk!' Thoughts on Reading Early Picture Books," pp. 64–69, traces his daughter's relationship to books from identification to story.

Annie Pissard, "Long Live Babar!," pp. 70–77, discusses the Brunhoffs' work in conjunction with an exhibition of original art for the books.

Jack Zipes, "A Second Gaze at Little Red Riding Hood's Trials and Tribulations," pp. 78–109, his radically different psychological approach includes much analysis of different versions of the illustrations over the years as well as of the story.

John Cech, "Remembering Caldecott: *The Three Jovial Huntsmen* and the Art of the Picture Book," pp. 110–119, a detailed analysis and appreciation.

Morton N. Cohen, "Another Wonderland: Lewis Carroll's *The Nursery Alice*," pp. 120–126, some notes on a more picture book-type version of *Alice* with color illustrations.

Leonard S. Marcus, "Picture Book Animals: How Natural a History?," pp. 127–139, analyzes the use of animal characters in picture books by types and discusses their relation to real animals.

Julie Hirsch, "Photography in Children's Books: A Generic Approach," pp. 140–155, gives examples and discusses how successfully they seem to meet the needs of the story.

Elizabeth Cleaver, "Idea to Image: The Journey of a Picture Book," pp. 156–170, covers her interest in Indian legends and details her work on *The Loon's Necklace*.

Nancy Willard, "The Birds and the Beasts were There: An Interview with Martin Provensen," pp. 171–183, gives background on the Provensens' life today, how they work, and how they came to picture books.

189. Lionni, Leo. "Before Images." *Horn Book* 60, no. 6 (November–December, 1984): 727–734.

The picture book as "the door that leads into the complexities of literacy." The need for the illustrator to rediscover childhood experiences, because "every work of art contains fragments of this journey." Feelings are a basic component to work for.

190. *Lively Art of Picture Books* (16mm film).   Weston, Connecticut: Weston Woods, no date (mid-1960?). 57 min.

An appreciation, including an animation of Keats' *Snowy Day*, a comparison of the works of 36 "outstanding artists," interviews on their work with Robert McCloskey, Barbara Cooney and Maurice Sendak, and an adaptation of McCloskey's *Time of Wonder*.

191. Lorraine, Walter. "The Art of the Picture Book." *Wilson Library Bulletin* 52, no. 2 (October, 1977): 144–147.

His introduction to a special issue laments the lack of content in the picture books that currently have better art than ever, defines picture books, gives some history and looks to the future.

192. MacCann, Donnarae. "Something Old, Something New: Children's Picture Books in Poland." *Wilson Library Bulletin* 52, no. 10 (June, 1978): 776–782.

Includes some history and critical analysis of the picture book art, its relation to the "fine art" world, and its importance in the books.

193. ———, and Olga Richard. *The Child's First Books: A Critical Study of Pictures and Texts*. New York: H.W. Wilson, 1973. 135pp.

Refreshingly free from cant, this book respects the esthetic capacities of children and seeks out examples of illustrators that contain "many particular beauties of art." A very short "Historical Perspective" is followed by an even shorter section on "Stereotypes." The bulk of the book is devoted to demonstrating the graphic elements and aspects of book design as well as to pay specific attention to Outstanding Contemporary Illustrators. The many b & w illustrations and several color reproductions are particularly well printed.

* Mahony, Bertha E.; Louise Payson Latimer; and Beulah Folmsbee, compilers. *Illustrators of Children's Books, 1744–1945.* Cited above as item 41.

194. Marantz, Kenneth. "The Picture Book as Art Object: A Call for Balanced Reviewing." *Wilson Library Bulletin* 52, no. 2 (October, 1977): 148–151.

Deplores the lack of attention to the picture book as a "form of visual art" rather than only literature.

195. ———. "The Picture Book: Bridge from Potter to Picasso." *Prelude Tapes* Series 7 (Audiotape). New York: Children's Book Council, 1983. 30 min.

Using a broad selection of recent picture books, Marantz analyzes their components and qualities (sequence, craftsmanship, design, styles, etc.) to make the case for their classification as art objects with strong esthetic content.

196. McGee, Lea M., and Gail E. Tompkins. "Wordless Picture Books Are For Older Readers too." *Journal of Reading* 27, no. 2 (November, 1983): 120–123.

Of interest for its list of wordless books that appeal to older students and its list of references. The books are used only as tools for teaching reading skills here. No art criticism or analysis.

197. Miller, Bertha Mahony; Ruth Viguers; and Marcia Dalphin, compilers. *Illustrators of Children's Books, 1946–1956.* Boston: Horn Book, 1958. 299pp.

Some b & w illustrations. Part I, "Eleven Years of Illustration in Children's Books," includes: "Distinction in Picture Books" by Marcia Brown, her critical words, pp. 2–12; "The Book Artist:

Ideas and Techniques" by Lynd Ward, pp. 14–35, his analysis of the current state of the art and its development during the years covered; "The European Picture Book" by Fritz Eichenberg, pp. 36–57, a personal report country by country of his observations. Part II, "Biographies," pp. 60–203, lists illustrators alphabetically with brief biographical notes and quotations. Part III, "Bibliographies," pp. 206–292, lists those active 1946–1956 with their works. See Bertha E. Mahony for earlier volume and Lee Kingman for later volumes in this series.

*   Morris, Charles Henry. *The Illustration of Children's Books.* Cited above as item 46.

198.   Moss, Elaine. *Picture Books for Young People, 9–13.* Rev. ed. (A Signal Bookguide.) Lockwood, England: Thimble Press, 1985. 46pp.

An annotated bibliography with a fresh point of view of picture books challenging enough for older students.

*   Moynihan, William T., and Mary E. Shaner, eds. *Masterworks of Children's Literature, Volume Eight: The Twentieth Century.* Cited above as item 47.

199.   Munro, Eleanor C. "Children's Book Illustration." *Art News* 53 (December, 1954): 41–48.

A pull-out type "design portfolio" with many 3-inch to 4-inch b & w illustrations from the U.S. and abroad, a few historical but many contemporary. Munro contrasts "little adults" of the past with what she calls "Juvenile Art" of today. Selected examples from 1950–1954 by *Art News* editors show what they consider style becoming stereotyped, and borrowing superficial elements from modern art since Cezanne, or from Expressionism to try to teach new sensitivity, "new patterns of thinking." Mention of study at Bank Street School on children's preferences.

200. Myatt, Barbara, and Juliet Mason Carter. "Picture Preferences of Children and Young Adults." *Educational Communication and Technology* 27, no.1 (Spring, 1979): 45–53.

Reviews some previous studies, discusses difficulties of research in this area. Uses six categories from photographs and line drawings through cartoon and collage. In this study children seem to prefer color photographs and "realism."

201. Nodelman, Perry. "How Children Respond to Art." *School Library Journal* 31, no. 4 (December, 1984): 40–41.

Nodelman's thesis is that children must be taught artistic conventions if they are to learn to value art of all kinds. He uses Burton's *Mike Milligan and his Steam Shovel* to point out 13 conventions used in the illustrations, ways of representing nature most adults have come to understand but which children need help with.

202. ———. "How Picture Books Work." *Proceedings of the Eighth Annual Conference of the Children's Literature Association.* University of Minnesota, March, 1981. Pp. 57–68.

Explains the relationship between text and illustrations generally. Uses the *Snow White* fairy tale, as visualized by Hyman and Burkert, as specific examples to point out the complex possibilities of illustrations as well as to make a case for Nodelman's bias about the best kind of illustration.

203. Packard, Myrna. "Some Second Graders' Verbal Responses to the Picturebook as Art Object." M.A. Thesis, Ohio State University, Columbus, 1984. 80pp.

A study that focuses on the esthetic qualities of picture books. Results suggest that these artifacts offer better vehicles to enhance esthetic development than the objects (usually reproductions of paintings) that are currently used.

204. Paulin, Mary Ann. *Creative Uses of Children's Literature.*
      Hamden, Connecticut: Library Professional Publication/Shoe
      String, 1982. 730pp.

      Chapter One, "Introducing Books All Kinds of Ways," includes
      techniques of presenting and promoting picture books; for
      example, pp. 37–44 cover "Choosing picture books for reading
      aloud," "Hints for reading picture books," "Picture books about
      pigs," etc.
      Chapter Two, "Experiencing Art Through Picture Books," is a
      hodgepodge collection of topics (categories) invented by the author
      which permits her to give annotations of several titles per topic
      and to offer a few suggestions for classroom activities. An author
      index lists 5,045 items. There are also Title and Subject Indexes.
      She also lists 785 nonprint titles in a Multi-media Index.

205. *Picture Book Design Conference: From Conception to
      Consumption.* Proceedings of a conference co-sponsored by the
      Ohio Arts Council and the Art Education Department of the
      Ohio State University, May 18–19, 1984. 91pp.

      Includes "An Editor's Comments" by Steven Roxburgh, pp. 3–
      10, analyzing the people, processes and some problems involved
      in putting together picture books; "A Publisher Adds to the
      Dialog" by David Godine, pp. 10–21, in which he discusses some
      of his publishing decisions and the design of some of his
      publications; "Ava Weiss and Vera Williams," pp. 21–36, where
      the author and the editor talk about their roles and how they work
      together, and Williams discusses her work on some specific
      books; "Leonard Everett Fisher," pp. 36–47, discusses how he
      works on both his paintings and his picture books; "Irene Haas,"
      pp. 47–54, covering how she develops a book in detail, and her
      experience at the printer with *Little Moon Theater*; "David
      Macaulay," pp. 54–65, chiefly detailing his work on the brain in
      The Amazing Garden. Also included are questions following each
      presentation and a general discussion and questions including all
      participants.

206. *Picture Books: Elements of Illustration and Story.*
(Videocassette.) Chicago: American Library Association, 1987.
25 min.

Betsy Hearne uses two editions of *The Easter Bunny that
Overslept* to compare Adrienne Adams' illustrations and other
visual aspects of the versions for the "illustration" part of her
presentation. Shows how the differences can affect the readings of
the text.

207. Pitz, Henry Clarence. *A Treasury of American Book
Illustration.* New York: Watson-Guptill, 1947. 128pp.

Chiefly illustrations, some in color. Some notes on the nature
and growth of illustration, on "Pictures for Children," pp. 15–17,
and on the design of the book and its jacket. Pp. 27–128 are all
examples.

208. Polette, Nancy. *"E" Is for Everybody: A Manual for Bringing
Fine Picture Books into the Hands and Hearts of Children.*
Metuchen, New Jersey: Scarecrow, 1976. 147pp.

An annotated bibliography of selected picture books includes
little analysis of illustration in the summary, but lists related
activities for each book. Part Two, pp. 87–142, describes art and
craft activities for children to use to interpret literature.

209. _____. *Picture Books for Gifted Programs.* Metuchen, New
Jersey: Scarecrow, 1981. 220pp.

Some b & w illustrations. Using many examples, Polette builds
from Piaget's theory of cognitive development activities and
examples for selected picture books. On pp. 23–29 she gives us a
taxonomy of visual communication skills for children from
kindergarten through high school and then an annotated list of
picture books for teaching the specific skills. Other lists are
included in chapters on communication skills, productive thinking
and critical thinking. Part Two moves from picture books to other
books to continue the development of critical thinking.

210. Prince, Diana M. "Heightening the Perceptive Abilities of Middle School Art Students Through the Use of the Picturebook." M.A. Thesis, Ohio State University, Columbus, 1985. 156pp.

Case studies demonstrating the use of picture books as the focus of study (both analytical and productive) in art classes of adolescents. Results were positive enough to warrant serious consideration of extending the study of picture books in art curriculums at all age levels.

211. Purves, Alan C., and Dianne L. Monson. *Experiencing Children's Literature*. Glenview, Illinois: Scott, Foresman, 1984. 216pp.

Some "b & w" illustrations are really sepia. "The role of the picture book in developing a sense of style," pp. 107–118, analyzes what a picture book is, and how the media used may convey the aim of the illustrator and the author. Influence of "Fine" art discussed. "Evaluating book illustration," pp. 156–164, asks some questions which may help analyze and judge. Includes picture books in other discussions, especially on poetry.

212. Ramsey, Inez L. "Effect of Art Style on Children's Picture Preferences." *Journal of Educational Research* 75, no. 4 (March–April, 1982): 237–240.

Preferences measured and correlated by how they related to text and by sex of child. Pictures used were in "photographic," "representational," "cartoon" and "expressionistic" styles as produced by professional artists from specific photographs, as opposed to actual illustrations from picture books. These were put with selected literary passages. Then children were either shown the picture first and asked which they would most like to read about, or they listened to the passage and were then asked which illustration "went" best with the story.

213. Read, Donna, and Henrietta M. Smith. "Teaching Visual Literacy Through Wordless Picture Books." *The Reading Teacher* (May, 1982): 930–933.

Covers the elements of line and shape, color and symbolism with examples from the books. Discusses their use with young and older children to teach sequencing, finding the main idea, making inferences and drawing conclusions, determining cause and effect and making judgments all from the pictures alone. Useful list of references included.

214. Richard, Olga. "The Visual Language of the Picture Book." *Wilson Library Bulletin* 44, no. 4 (December, 1969): 435–447.

A detailed exposition of the qualities of the illustrations that need to be evaluated in picture books. Analyzes the elements of color, line, shape, texture, composition, plus those specific to the art of the book such as binding, end papers, the type and its placement. Discusses the personal role of the artist. Gives many examples for each element, with some b & w illustrations.

215. Roads, Clarice. *Exploring the Art of Picture Books.* Oklahoma State Department of Education, 1982. 53pp.

A guide for teachers which includes a list of books and illustrators, and plans of many related activities for grades K–3 and 4–8. A *really* useful bibliography includes sections on art techniques as well as books and media for the adult and the child.

216. Robinson, Evelyn Rose, ed. *Readings About Children's Literature.* New York: David McKay, 1966. 431pp.

Reprints include Anne Carroll Moore, "Illustrating Books for Children," pp. 195–201, analyzing some of her favorite illustrators; Maurice Sendak, "The Shape of Music," pp. 201–205, telling how he works with music in mind to make the art "quicken." Mentions other illustrators whose work he admires. Madel Rudisill, "Children's Preferences for Color Versus Other Qualities in Illustration," pp. 205–214, a study of children's preferences in grades K–6 in Kentucky. There are notes on illustration and/or art on p. 77 and p. 237, and on illustration in informational books, pp. 377–378 and pp. 390–391.

217. Ryder, John. *Artists of a Certain Line: A Selection of Illustrators for Children's Books.* London: Bodley Head, 1960. 128pp.

Brief biographies (single page plus facing page illustration) of 40 artists picked for their talents in drawing. The very personal introduction discusses the qualities which are necessary for a superior illustration. Fully illustrated with b & w historical and contemporary examples.

218. Saxby, H.M. *A History of Australian Children's Literature, 1841–1941.* Sidney: Wentworth Books, 1969. 212pp.

"Books with pictures," p. 120, gives brief mention of pictures. "The Influence in Australia of Art Nouveau," pp. 121–124, shows the style's influence on the illustrated book.

219. Schuman, Patricia. "Concerned Criticism or Casual Cop-Out?" *School Library Journal* 18 (January, 1972): 21–24, and *Library Journal* 97, no. 2 (January 15, 1972): 245–248.

Analyzes the sources of reviews and criticism of books for children available to concerned adults seeking guidance, showing the scarcity and difficulty of finding this. Calls attention to the roles of children and young adults as consumers whose input should be considered.

220. Schwarcz, Joseph H. *Ways of the Illustrator: Visual Communication in Children's Literature.* Chicago: American Library Association, 1982. 202pp.

A thoughtful attempt to answer the two major questions set for itself: "In what ways does the illustration...express its contents and meanings?" and "How does the illustration relate to the verbal text?" Both themes and elements of artistic composition are employed with examples drawn from several countries as well as through many comparisons of a single story illustrated by different artists. Emphasis on current books. Illustrated books are accepted and treated as art objects.

221. Sheppard, Valerie. "Give All Ages a Look at a Mother Goose Book." ERIC Microfiche ED 218604 82. 9pp.

Paper presented at the Texas State Council Conference of the International Reading Association, El Paso, March 11–13, 1982. The different illustrators and their styles covered are Rojankovsky, Wildsmith, Jeffers, Spier, Galdone, Lobel and the Provensens. Bibliography.

222. Shulevitz, Uri. "What is a Picture Book?" *Wilson Library Bulletin* 55, no. 2 (October, 1980): 99–101.

". . . A picture book is unclear or incomplete without the pictures," with examples.

*   _____. *Writing with Pictures: How to Write and Illustrate Children's Books.* Cited above as item 91.

223. Smith, Irene. *A History of the Newbery and Caldecott Medals.* New York: Viking, 1957. 140pp.

No illustration except of medals. Details the people involved and the events that led to the establishment of the awards. Also some discussion of the award events. The chapter on award-winning books and their continual popularity, pp. 93–101, discusses the Caldecott winners, giving brief descriptions and possible reasons for their popularity.

224. Smith, James A., and Dorothy M. Park. *Word Music and Word Magic: Children's Literature Methods.* Boston: Allyn and Bacon, 1977. 564pp.

Some b & w photographs and illustrations. "Picture Books, Picture-Story Books and Illustrated Books" are briefly treated in pp. 28–30. In chapters on "Classical Illustrators," pp. 219–235, and "Modern Illustrators," pp. 236–267, many articles about illustrators and the use of their works with children are excerpted and commented upon, as are several illustrators in the chapter, "New Models, New Faces," pp. 192–218.

225. Smith, James Steel. *A Critical Approach to Children's Literature.* New York: McGraw-Hill, 1967. 442pp.

B & w illustrated examples. Chapter 12, "To read, to look," pp. 305–342, discusses the importance of the visual image for the child. Gives a brief history of illustration. Covers effects of Modern Art, Representational Art, Disney School, Seuss and other comics, abstraction and trends in layout, printing and relating illustration to text. Gives many examples plus a long list of illustrators and their work.

226. Smith, Nicole Gnezda. "Aesthetic Literacy: Teaching Preschool Children to Respond to Book Illustrations." M.A. Thesis, Ohio State University, Columbus, 1981. 76pp.

The author defines "aesthetic literacy" as the ability to "read" pictures, to become sensitive to the visual qualities of colors, textures, shapes, etc. She points to the need for preschool education from her research findings that at this age children do respond aesthetically to pictures and that this capacity can be enhanced through education.

227. Soriano, Marc. *Guide de Litterature pour la Jeunesse: Courants, Problemes, Choix, d'Auteurs.* Paris: Flammarion, 1975. 568pp.

This general dictionary of children's literature has a discussion of illustration on pp. 326–336 with psychological role of the image in education. A general history ends with the role of the mass media and the improvement in the technical process of reproduction. On pp. 439–453 "Research and criticism in the field of children's literature" discusses the problem of approaching and appreciating art destined for children and the inadequacy of most criticism. Some French illustrators are included in the dictionary format.

228. St. John, Judith. "The Osborne Collection of Early Children's Books: Highlights in Retrospect." *Horn Book* 60 (September–October, 1984): 652–660.

The retiring head of the Osborne Collection describes the collection and its growth, including key acquisitions and publications.

229. Stewig, John Warren. "Alphabet Books: A Neglected Genre." *Language Arts* (January, 1978): 6–11.

Shows how to use these books to help develop visual and verbal skills with children, giving many examples.

230. ———. *Book Illustration: Key to Visual and Verbal Literacy*. Paper presented at the Annual Meeting of the International Reading Association, New York City, May 13–16, 1975. ERIC Document ED 112352. 11pp.

Discusses the subskills of visual and verbal literacy: describing, comparing and oral valuing; i.e., "prefer or like." Uses versions of "Red Riding Hood," "Cinderella," "Mother Goose," and the "Owl and the Pussycat."

231. ———. *Children and Literature*. Chicago: Rand McNally, 1980. 562pp.

Many b & w and a few color illustrations. Space devoted shows the attention to picture books. Chapter Two "Studying Book Illustration," pp. 38–73, emphasizes the importance of illustration and the artist, with a discussion of related art movements. Chapter Three, pp. 74–95, covers "The Alphabet Book," purposes, types and evaluation. Chapter Four, "Picture Books," pp. 96–129, analyzes, evaluates and discusses children's responses. Chapter Five, pp. 130–158, is a discussion and analysis of wordless picture books. Bibliographies of examples and of sources of further information.

232. _____. "Children's Preference in Picture Book Illustration." *Educational Leadership* 30, no.3 (December, 1972): 273–277.

Stewig reviewed 16 studies designed to assess children's preferences in pictures and found them all to be erroneous or inconclusive. He concludes that picture books are chosen primarily by means of "simple intuition" and asks if better research methods might provide less idiosyncratic bases for choice.

233. _____. "Picture Books: What Do Reviews Really Review?" *Top of the News* 37 (Fall, 1980): 83–84.

Briefly examines reviews of picture books in four "widely respected" sources during 1979 to tally percentage of words describing visual aspects. Deplores low percentage as indicative of lack of attention to this most important aspect.

234. _____. "Trends in Caldecott Award Winners." *Elementary English* 45 (February, 1968): 218–223, 260.

A careful analysis of both winners and honor books over 30 years as to "realism quotient" to see whether in these books at least there was a trend toward or away from realism, and any trends to or from certain media. There seems to be "An increasing willingness . . . to depart from the traditional. . . ."

   *   *Story of a Book* (Sound Filmstrip). Cited above as item 94.

235. Stott, Jon C. *Children's Literature from A to Z: A Guide for Parents and Teachers.* New York: McGraw-Hill, 1984. 318pp.

34 small b & w page-spread illustrations. Dictionary-form reference tool covering general terms, themes and important people in Children's Literature. Entries run from less than one page to more than two in the case of "Picture books and illustration." Biographical and critical information on over fifty

picture book artists are included under their individual names. "Tips for parents and teachers" follow each entry.

236. Sutherland, Zena, and May Hill Arbuthnot. *Children and Books.* Seventh ed. Glenview, Illinois: Scott, Foresman, 1986. 768pp.

Illustrated in b & w and color. Chapter 5, pp. 80–129, "Books for the Very Young," discusses picture books with critical comments. Chapter 6, pp. 132–162, "Artists and Children's Books," also has critical comments as it discusses particular artists.

237. _____, and Betsy Hearne. "In Search of the Perfect Picture Book Definition." *Wilson Library Bulletin* 52, no. 2 (October, 1977): 158–160.

Many examples are given to support a range of picture books to show how the pictures should "either dominate the text or are as important."

238. Townsend, John Rowe. *Written for Children: An Outline of English-Language Children's Literature.* Revised. Philadelphia: Lippincott, 1965, 1974. 368pp.

A history and analysis of the types of literature, including picture books. Some b & w illustrations. Pages 308–320, "Picture Books in Bloom," discuss the U.S. scene. Pages 321–330 cover picture books in Britain.

The author is concerned that the reviewers don't have the qualifications to review picture books while art critics have generally not become involved, leading to less satisfactory reviewing.

239. Warthman, John Burns. "A Study of Picture Preferences of Caldecott Award Winners and Runners-up by Fourth, Fifth, and Sixth Grade Children of Selected Schools." University of Southern Mississippi, 1970. University Microfilm No. 71–13, 589.

582 children in grades four, five and six made choices from 28 Caldecott Award and honor books, and selected the Award book for only two of the seven years sampled.

240. Watanabe, Shigeo. "Japanese and American Picture Books...Similarities and Differences." *Michigan Librarian* 37 (Winter, 1971): 11–14.

After a brief history, discusses several modern Japanese illustrators, including Nakatani, Akaba, Segawa. Problem in Japan of well-educated children having quality books and poorer children having the gaudy. Watanabe feels that American books have more humor and fantasy, Japanese parents' views have more importance, and that values differ in the two cultures.

241. Watts, Lynne, and John Nisbet. *Legibility in Children's Books: A Review of Research*. New York: Humanities, 1972. England: NFER Publishing Co. Ltd. 104pp.

Discusses the effect on the young reader of various aspects of book design, such as type, margins, paper. Section 4 "Color and Illustration," pp. 70–86, treats size, position and nature of pictures. Includes examples and illustrations.

242. Weller, Joan. "Sophisticated Picturebooks." *Canadian Library Journal* 41, no. 1 (February, 1984): 21–24.

Comments on the quality of recent picture books. Higher quality of color is made possible by new technology and has produced a "New Breed" for an older child, reflecting a variety of art movements.

243. Whalen-Levitt, Peggy. "Picture Play in Children's Books: A Celebration of Visual Awareness." *Wilson Library Bulletin* 55, no. 2 (October, 1980): 102–107.

Gives examples of images in picture books that challenge our expectations or offer allusions or parodies beyond the story.

244. White, Mary Lou. *Children's Literature: Criticism and Response.* Columbus, Ohio: Charles E. Merrill, 1976. 252pp.

Reprints of works appearing elsewhere. Uses a framework of four theories of criticism: psychological, sociological, archetypical and structural. Includes activities for children. Patricia Cianciolo, "Use Wordless Picture Books . . . ," and Rose Agree, "Lionni's Artichokes: An Interview," are the only selections dealing with picture books. These articles appear in separate annotations further in this document.

245. Williams, Clarence M., and John L. Debes, eds. *Proceedings of the First National Conference on Visual Literacy.* New York: Pitman, 1970. 295pp.

Since "Visual Literacy" is a term used by some critics of picture books, this volume is helpful in clarifying the many meanings of the term, although it does not deal anywhere with picture books directly. Almost 50 pages cover concepts, research, and programs in the schools, including teacher preparation. Of particular interest is "Design in Communication," pp. 36–41, by Donis A. Dondis, which tries to show that we receive messages from our visual associations with basic shapes.

246. Yeager, Allan. *Using Picture Books with Children: A Guide to Owlet Books.* New York: Holt, Rinehart and Winston, 1973. 203pp.

For each of 61 Owlet books, Yeager summarizes the story, discusses the illustrations very briefly and relates them to the text. He also gives other information and suggestions for the teacher working with students and the book. The illustrators included are listed in the index.

247. Zerfoss, Charlotte. "The Picture Book: Art for Children." *Drexel Library Quarterly* 12, no. 4 (October, 1976): 12–19.

Brief paragraphs pointing out a string of qualities illustrations should possess: free of stereotype, skilled draftsmanship, style adapted to the narrative, etc. Uses a score of examples as models of qualities.

PART IV

Artists Anthologized

* Alderman, Belle, and Lauren Harman, eds. *The Imagineers: Writing and Illustrating Children's Books.* Cited above as item 99.

248. *The Artist and the Child: Exhibition of Children's Books and Original Illustration from the John D. Merriam Collection.* Boston: Public Library, 1980. 96pp.

Chiefly b & w illustrations from the exhibition. Brief biographical sketches of the 62 illustrators are included.

* Bader, Barbara. *American Picturebooks from Noah's Ark to the Beast Within.* Cited above as item 4.

249. *Biennale of Illustrations Bratislava.* Bratislava: Mlade leta, published after the two biennales 1967 and 1969, and 1971 and 1973.

These profusely illustrated catalogs in color contain prize-winning illustrations and brief information on the illustrators in several languages including english. More recent catalogs cover single biennales and are not in english.

250. Bolton, Theodore. *American Book Illustrators: Bibliographic Checklists of 123 Artists.* New York: Bowker, 1938. 290pp.

Some earlier American illustrators of children's books (e.g., Lynd Ward, N. C. Wyeth, Kurt Wiese, Helen Sewell, Howard Pyle, the Petershams, Robert Lawson, Wanda Gag, James Daugherty, Gelett Burgess, Boris Artzybasheff, Valenti Angelo) are included in this alphabetical listing along with places where the illustrations are published.

251. Butler, Francelia, and Richard Rotert, eds. *Reflections on Literature for Children.* Hamden, Connecticut: Library Professional Publications, 1984. 281pp. Selected from *Children's Literature Annual.*

Roger Sale, "Child Reading and Man Reading; Oz, Babar and Pooh," pp. 19–31, includes discussion of relationship between De Brunhoff's words and pictures. Seth Sicroff, "Prickles Under the Frock: The Art of Beatrix Potter," pp. 39–44, includes relation of illustrations to text. Michael Patrick Hearn, "Mr. Ruskin and Miss Greenaway," pp. 182–190, briefly analyzes his relationship with her as well as her life and work. Jennifer R. Waller, "Maurice Sendak and the Blakean Vision of Childhood," pp. 260–268, compares the two and shows Blake's influence on Sendak. Analyzes both art and language of Sendak's books in this light.

252. Carpenter, Humphrey, and Mari Richard. *The Oxford Companion to Children's Literature.* New York: Oxford University Press, 1984. 586pp.

Occasional small b & w reproductions and 26 photos. Very comprehensive although uneven and with British-emphasis treatment of the entire field, in dictionary format with extensive cross-references. Includes important subjects and characters from books and other media in english plus those from other countries that have become part of our culture. Greenaway and Potter are given several pages, while E.J. Keats rates only one paragraph.

253. Cech, John, ed. *American Writers for Children, 1900–1960.* (Dictionary of Literary Biography, vol. 22.) Detroit: Gale, 1983. 412pp.

Photographic portraits and b & w reproductions of works. Contains multi-page essays with biographical and critical comments, lists of works and further references, interviews, locations of papers. The picture book illustrators included are Bemelmans, M.W. Brown, Burton, the D'Aulaires, de Angeli, Ets, Gag, Gramatky, Lawson, Lenski, McCloskey, the Petershams, Rey, Thurber, Ward, and Garth Williams.

254. *Children's Book Showcase.* Catalogs of traveling exhibits sponsored yearly by the Children's Book Council, 67 Irving Place, New York, N.Y., 10003, in the 1970's.

The books were selected by a committee. Each catalog lists the title with a small b & w reproduction, gives technical production details and a summary of the book for each included in the "showcase."

255. Commire, Anne, ed. *Something About the Author.* Detroit: Gale. Continuing publication.

Volumes 1–45 (1986) all include illustrations. Includes major writers and illustrators for children. Biographical and critical information is included, plus a list of works. A cumulative "Illustrations Index" precedes the Author Index. Before volume 15, only authors and illustrators alive in 1961 were included. Beginning with volume 15 "the time scope was broadened" to include some major authors who died before 1961, formerly in the editor's *Yesterday's Authors of Books for Children.*

256. _____. *Yesterday's Authors of Books for Children: Facts and Pictures about Authors and Illustrators of Books for Young People from Early Times to 1960.* Detroit: Gale, 1976 and 1978. Varying pages.

Two volumes. Illustrations are from books or from motion pictures of books. Includes biographies, criticism, quotations from diaries, illustration listed by illustrator; for example, Kate Greenaway, pp 129–141, volume 1 and Robert Lawson, pp. 222–241, volume 2.

257. *Contemporary American Illustrators of Children's Books*. New Brunswick, New Jersey: Rutgers University Press, 1974. 72pp.

Full b & w illustrations on each page facing artist's information. Catalog of an exhibition that travelled from Rutgers to four other museums during 1974–1975. Following a two-page essay by A. Hyatt Mayor, there is a page of biographical information, a quotation, and a list of illustrations for each artist. Contributing are Adrienne Adams, Erik Blegvad, Marcia Brown, Jean Charlot, Tony Chen, Barbara Cooney, James Daugherty, Harry Devlin, William Pene du Bois, Roger Duvoisin, Fritz Eichenberg, Antonio Frasconi, Don Freeman, Edward Gorey, Lorenzo Homar, Ezra Jack Keats, Blair Lent, Leo Lionni, Arnold Lobel, Joseph Low, Robert McCloskey, Evaline Ness, Peter Parnall, Leona Pierce, Ellen Raskin, John Schoenherr, Maurice Sendak, Marc Simont, Lynd Ward, Garth Williams, Taro Yashima, and Margot Zemach.

*   Cott, Jonathan. *Pipers at the Gates of Dawn: The Wisdom of Children's Literature*. Cited above as item 126.

258. Crouch, Marcus. *Treasure Seekers and Borrowers: Children's Books in Britain 1900–1960*. London: Library Association, 1962. 162pp.

Generally a chronological survey of all children's literature. Index is only of authors and titles, so his views on picture books and illustrators must be searched out in the text. Pages 134–138 discuss some contemporary illustrators.

259. Darling, Richard, L. *The Rise of Children's Book Reviewing in America, 1865–1881*. New York: Bowker, 1968. 452pp.

Some b & w illustrations. Describes the publishing at the time, the types of children's books, general criticism and some notes on reviewing. Then surveys literary monthly and other periodicals, including a chapter on children's periodicals. Includes bibliography of reviews and sample reviews. Finding criticism of picture books requires searching. There is no analysis of picture books. Greenaway and Caldecott are mentioned.

* Egoff, Sheila A., ed. *One Ocean Touching: Papers from the First Pacific Rim Conference on Children's Literature.* Cited above as item 142.

260. _____ et al. *Only Connect: Readings on Children's Literature.* 2nd ed. New York: Oxford University Press, 1980. 457pp.

Contains: Edward Ardizzone, "Creation of a picture book," from *Top of the News*, Dec. 1959. Roger Duvoisin, "Children's book illustration: the pleasures and problems," from *Top of the News*, Nov. 1965. Frederick Laws, "Randolph Caldecott," from *The Saturday Book*, no. 16 (Cupid Press). Walter Lorraine, "An interview with Maurice Sendak," from *Wilson Library Bulletin*, Oct. 1977.

261. Field, Elinor Whitney, ed. *Horn Book Reflections on Children's Books and Readings: Selected from Eighteen Years of the Horn Book Magazine, 1949–1966.* Boston: Horn Book, 1969. 367pp.

Includes: Warren Chappell, "Benchmarks for Illustrators of Children's Books," pp. 73–77. "There should be no such category as children's illustration"—i.e., good artist illustrators don't change hats for children—from Rembrandt, Daumier, Goya, etc., to Tenniel and Shepard (Oct. 1957). Henry C. Pitz, "The Art of Illustration," pp. 78–81. Summary of his impressions of foreign illustrations of the time (Oct. 1962), the editors in the United States, the quality of the field in general. Barbara Cooney, "An Illustrator's Viewpoint," pp. 82–85 (Feb. 1961). Impressions of the history, current production in the United States and abroad, and the importance of good design. Bettina Ehrlich, "Story and Picture in Children's Books," pp. 86–93. On illustration: how the child "reads" pictures and how to illustrate for them (Oct. 1952).

262. Freedman, Russell. *Holiday House: The First Fifty Years.* New York: Holiday House, 1985. 152pp.

B & w illustrations; several on most pages. The history of the firm includes anecdotes about the illustrators who worked with them, from Glen Rounds to Janet Stevens. Also including Tomie de Paola, Donna Diamond, Fritz Eichenberg, Leonard Everett Fisher, Gail Gibbons, Trina Schart Hyman, Steven Kroll, and Charles Mikolaycak among others. Complete year-by-year list of their publications with illustrators. The hundreds of b & w illustrations add to the carefully designed pages to produce a book both handsome and easily read.

263. Gankina, E. *Khudozhnik v Sovremennoi Detskoi Knige.* Moscow: Sovietski Khudozhnik, 1977. 215pp.

Includes b & w and color illustrations, and bibliography. Covers from the 1920's to the present. Many illustrations on every page, for examples even if you can't read the language.

264. Haviland, Virginia. *Children and Literature: Views and Reviews.* Glenview, Ill.: Scott Foresman, 1973. 461pp.

A few b & w illustrations. "A selection of essays, criticism, and statements of trends in the world of children's books...." First part (chapters 1–5) discusses the history of children's books, with some mention of illustrations.
Chapter 5, pp. 169–201, is "Illustrators and illustrations." Pages 169–172 are an introduction. Then it includes: Louise Seaman Bechtel, "The Art of Illustrating Books for the Younger Reader," pp. 173–176, reprinted from her book, *Books in Search of Children.* Summarizes history and mentions some noteworthy names. Roger Duvoisin, "Children's Book Illustration: The Pleasures and Problems," pp. 177–187, from *Top of the News* (Nov. 1965): 22–33. Discusses the role of illustrator, a painting as opposed to an illustration (including art history discussion) comparisons of illustrations (Dore vs. Derain of Rabelais' *Gargantua*), child's awareness. Maurice Sendak, "Mother Goose's Garnishings," pp. 188–195, from *Book Week* Fall Children's Issue, Oct. 31, 1965. Discusses versions, both verse and illustration, historically including Crane, Caldecott, Greenaway,

Brooke, Tudor, and, more contemporary, Reed, Wildsmith and Cooney, Low, Briggs. Page 196 has other reviews by Viguers and Heins. Crispin Fisher, "A Load of Old Nonsense, Edward Lear Resurrected by Four Publishers," pp. 198–201, from *Growing Point*, Nov. 1969. Criticism of versions of Lear with illustrations by Helen Oxenbury, Gerald Rose, Dale Maxey, Edward Gorey. Chapter 10, "The international scene," pp. 326–390, includes mention of the H.C. Andersen award, p. 329, list, p. 449, Australian picture books, p. 343, German picture books, pp. 345–347, 354, French, p. 355, Czech and Slovak, pp. 368–369. Chapter 12, "Awards," includes criteria for Caldecott medals and winners, pp. 416–431; Greenaway, pp. 447–448.

265. _____, ed. *The Openhearted Audience: Ten Authors Talk About Writing for Children*. Washington, D.C.: Library of Congress, 1980. 198pp.

Includes "Questions to an artist who is also an author," pp. 25–45, Maurice Sendak with Virginia Haviland. Biographical and bibliographic information, many b & w illustrations, and answers to a series of questions.

266. Hoffman, Miriam, and Eva Samuels. *Authors and Illustrators of Children's Books: Writings on Their Lives and Works*. New York: Bowker, 1972. 471pp.

Appendix lists english-language works of each. Includes a chapter on each of 50, almost half of whom are illustrators; all have some critical comments. All articles are reprinted from periodicals, newspapers, and journals with publication dates from 1950–1971 and have added editor's notes.
Illustrators include:
Ardizzone, Edward: "An autobiographical note," pp. 1–5.
Bemelmans, Ludwig: "The children's world of Ludwig Bemelmans," pages 6–18.
Burton, Virginia Lee: "Virginia Lee Burton's dynamic sense of design," pp. 41–55.

de Angeli, Marguerite L.: "Marguerite L. de Angeli: Faith in the human spirit," pp. 108–114.

Duvoisin, Roger: "Roger Duvoisin—Distinguished contributor to the world of children's literature," pp. 125–134.

Emberly, Ed: "The meteoric career of Ed Emberly," pp. 135–140.

Ets, Marie Hall: "Marie Hall Ets—Her picture storybooks," pp. 141–148.

Geisel, Theodor Seuss: "Who thunk you up Dr. Seuss?," pp. 165–171.

Gramatky, Hardy: "Little Toot—Hero," pp. 172–179.

Hader, Berta and Elmer Hader: "Berta and Elmer Hader," pp. 180–185.

Holling, Holling C.: "Holling C. Holling: author and illustrator," pp. 209–216.

Keats, Ezra Jack: "Ezra Jack Keats, author and illustrator," pp. 231–242.

Lawson, Robert: "Robert Lawson: author and illustrator," pp. 256–267.

Lenski, Lois: "Lois Lenski: Children's interpreter," pp. 268–274.

Lionni, Leo: "My books for children," pp. 302–307.

McCloskey, Robert: "Robert McCloskey: Master of humorous realism," pp. 308–326.

Milhous, Katherine: "Enjoying festivals with Katherine Milhous," pp. 327–339.

Politi, Leo: "To the children with love, from Leo Politi," pp. 348–352.

Rey, Margaret & H.A. Rey "Margaret & H.A. Rey," pp. 359–363.

Sendak, Maurice: "Questions to an artist who is also an author," pp. 364–377.

Ward, Lynd: "Mary McNeer Ward and Lynd Ward," pp. 403–406.

Wildsmith, Brian: "Antic Disposition," pp. 412–416.

267. Hopkins, Lee Bennett. *Books are by People: Interviews with 104 Authors and Illustrators of Books for Young Children.* New York: Citation, 1969. 349pp.

Small b & w photographs of the people. Several pages on each entry include some biographical information, a discussion of the persons and how they live, and some information on their work.

268. Horn Book Magazine. *Horn Book Sampler on Children's Books and Reading: Selected from Twenty-Five Years of The Horn Book Magazine, 1924-1948.* Boston: Horn Book, 1959. 261pp.

Part I, "How the story happened," includes "About Lucy and Tom" by Edward Ardizzone from the March, 1938 issue.

Part II, "Let us now praise artists!," includes: "Flowers for a Birthday—Kate Greenaway, Mar. 17, 1846" by Anne Parish, with notes on life and work, from March, 1946.

"Arthur Rackham and *The Wind in the Willows*" by George Macy, life and art, from the May, 1940 issue.

"The Genius of Arthur Rackham" by Robert Lawson, an appreciation of his art from the May, 1940 issue.

"Leslie Brooke: pied piper of English picture books" by Anne Carroll Moore, who met him, from the March 1925 issue.

"Leslie Brooke" by Anne Carroll Moore, with his comments on other books, from the May, 1941 issue.

"A Publisher's Odyssey" by Esther Averill; her experiences with Rojankovsky, from the Sept. and Dec., 1938, and the Feb., 1939 issues.

"Illustrations Today in Children's Books" by Warren Chappell, discussing the art and technology involved, from the Nov. 1941 issue.

Part VII, "Small Children and Books," includes: "A Canadian Tribute to Leslie Brooke" by Lillian H. Smith from the May, 1941 issue.

"Beatrix Potter and her Nursery Classics" by Bertha Mahoney Miller from the May, 1941 issue.

Alice Dalgliesh on children's choices from the August, 1933 issue, updated in 1959.

269. Hyland, Douglas. *Howard Pyle and the Wyeths: Four Generations of American Imagination.* Memphis, Tenn.: Memphis Brooks Museum of Art, 1983. 104pp.

Many b & w and a few color illustrations. Published in conjunction with the exhibition held at the Memphis Brooks Museum of Art, Sept. 1 to Oct. 23, 1983; Montgomery Museum of Fine Arts, Nov. 12, 1983 to Jan. 2, 1984; North Carolina Museum of Art, Feb. 4 to April 1, 1984. Introductory essays cover the lives of the artists and give some criticism of their work. Their illustrations for children are included but not treated separately.

270. *Illustrating in the Third Dimension: The Artist Turned Craftsman.* Society of Illustrators, Library of American Illustration. Volume 1. Edited by Howard Munce, designed by Robert Geissman. New York: Hastings House, 1978. 112pp.

Chiefly b & w and color photographs of three-dimensional work. Two or three pages on each illustrator include examples of work plus biographical information and comments by the artist. Artists include Leo and Diane Dillon, Caldecott winners.

271. *Illustrators of Children's Books.* Published yearly in conjunction with the Bologna International Children's Bookfair.

Catalog of invited artists with examples of work and biographical information. From 1980 to present available.

 *   Jacques, Robin. *Illustrators at Work.* Cited above as item 85.

272. Jan, Isabelle. *On Children's Literature.* Translated from the French. Edited by Catherine Storr. London: Allen Lane, 1973. 189pp.

Only a brief mention of Maurice Sendak, and of Beatrix Potter's animal pictures.

273. Jones, Cornelia. *British Children's Authors: Interviews at Home.* Chicago: A.L.A. 1976. 176pp.

Includes some biographical information, some quotations, which are mainly answers to questions, and bibliographies, some annotated. Illustrators are Victor G. Ambrus, pp. 11–19; Edward Ardizzone, pp. 21–29; Charles Keeping, pp. 101–113; and Brian Wildsmith, pp. 155–166. Illustrated.

274. Jones, Dolores Blythe. *Children's Literature Awards and Winners: A Directory of Prizes, Authors and Illustrators.* Detroit: Gale, 1983. 495pp.

Part I, "Directory of awards," gives full information on awards, criteria, history, etc., plus bibliographical information on winners and runners-up.
Part II, "Award-winning authors and illustrators," lists all recipients alphabetically with awards won.
Part III, "Selected bibliography," lists relevant books, chapters, journal articles, dissertations, reports. First edition supplement, 1984, updates all awards through May 31, 1984 and includes 32 new awards.
"Subject List of Awards" includes "Illustration."

* Jones, Linda Harris. *A Comparison of the Works of Walter Crane, Randolph Caldecott and Kate Greenaway and their Contributions to Children's Literature.* Cited above as item 36.

* Kingman, Lee; Joanna Foster; and Ruth Giles Lontoft, compilers. *Illustrations of Children's Books, 1957–1966.* Cited above as item 175.

* _____; Grace Allen Hogarth; and Harriet Quimby, compilers. *Illustrators of Children's Books, 1967–1976.* Cited above as item 176.

275. _____. *Newbery and Caldecott Medal Books: 1956–1965.* With acceptance papers, biographies and related materials chiefly from the *Horn Book Magazine.* Boston: Horn Book, 1965. 300pp.

Caldecott award information from page 163. Artists covered include Feodor Rojankovsky, speech pp. 166–170; "Unfinished Portrait of an Artist," by Esther Averill, pp. 171–175.

Marc Simont, speech pp. 177–179; "Marc Simont," by Elizabeth Lansing, pp. 180–186.

Robert McCloskey, speech pp. 194–195; "Bob McCloskey, Inventor" by Marc Simont, pp. 196–197.

Barbara Cooney, speech pp. 199–202; "Barbara Cooney," by Anna Newton Porter, pp. 203–207.

Marie Hall Ets, speech pp. 209–211; "Marie Hall Ets," by May Massee, pp. 212–216.

Nicolas Sidjakov, speech pp. 218–220; "Nicolas Sidjakov," pp. 221–224.

Marcia Brown, speech pp. 226–231; "From Caldecott to Caldecott," pp. 232–237.

Ezra Jack Keats, speech pp. 239–240; "Ezra Jack Keats," by Esther Hautzig, pp. 241–245.

Maurice Sendak, speech pp. 247–253; "Maurice Sendak," by Leo Wolfe, pp. 254–257.

Beni Montresor, speech pp. 259–265; "Beni Montresor," pp. 266–269.

"Picture Books Today," by Norma R. Fryett, pp. 270–280, a description and appreciation of the winners; and a list of honor books and a b & w insert with illustrations from each winner are also included.

276. _____. *Newbery and Caldecott Medal Books: 1966–1975.* With acceptance papers, biographies and related materials chiefly from the *Horn Book Magazine.* Boston: Horn Book, 1975. 321pp.

Caldecott information from page 155, with color illustrations from the medal books and b & w portrait photographs.

Artists are: Nonny Hogrogian, speech pp. 179–180; "Nonny Hogrogian," by John Paul Itta, pp. 181–185.

Evaline Ness, speech pp. 186–191; "Ealine Ness," by Ann Durell, pp. 192–198.

Ed Emberly, speech pp. 199–204; "Ed Emberly," by Barbara Emberly, pp. 205–207.

Uri Shulevitz, speech pp. 209–213; "Uri Shulevitz," by Marjorie Zaum, pp. 214–216.

William Steig, speech pp. 218–219; "William Steig," by Robert Kraus, pp. 220–222.

Gail E. Haley, speech pp. 223–228, note pp. 229–231; "Gail E. Haley," by Arnold Arnold, pp. 232–235.

Nonny Hogrogian, speech "How the Caldecott Changed My Life—Twice," pp. 237–239; "Nonny Hogrogian," by David Kherdian, pp. 240–242.

Blair Lent, speech pp. 244–249; "Blair Lent," by William Sleator, pp. 250–255.

Margot Zemach, speech pp. 257–259; Margot Zemach, by A.L. Lloyd, pp. 260–264.

Gerald McDermott, speech pp. 266–271; "Gerald McDermott," by Priscilla Moulton, pp. 272–275.

Also includes "Picture Books, Art and Illustration," by Barbara Bader, pp. 276–290, which describes the winners with appreciation, a list of the honor books and a discussion of honor books by Elizabeth Johnson, pp. 297–302, mentioning illustration in particular.

277. ———. *Newbery and Caldecott Medal Books: 1976–1985.* With acceptance papers, biographies and related materials chiefly from the *Horn Book Magazine.* Boston: Horn Book, 1986. 358pp.

Caldecott information begins on page 167. Artists are: Leo and Diane Dillon, speech pp. 170–174; "Leo and Diane Dillon," by Phyllis J. Fogelman, pp. 175–180, and speech pp. 181–187; "Diane Dillon," by Leo Dillon, pp. 188–189; "Leo Dillon," by Diane Dillon, pp. 190–191; "Leo and Diane Dillon," by Leo Dillon, pp. 191–192.

Peter Spier, speech pp. 193–200; "Peter Spier," by Janet D. Chenery, pp. 201–203.

Paul Goble, speech pp. 205–207; "Paul Goble," by Joseph Epes Brown, pp. 208–209.

Barbara Cooney, speech pp. 211–215; "Barbara Cooney," by Constance Reed McClellan, pp. 216–219.

Arnold Lobel, speech pp. 220–225; "Arnold Lobel," by Elizabeth Gordon, pp. 226–228.

Chris Van Allsburg, speech pp. 230–233; "Chris Van Allsburg," by David Macaulay, pp. 234–237.
Marcia Brown, speech pp. 239–249; "Marcia Brown," by Janet Loranger, pp. 250–253.
Alice and Martin Provensen, speech pp. 255–258; "Alice and Martin Provensen," by Nancy Willard, pp. 259–262.
Trina Schart Hyman, speech pp. 264–274; "Trina Schart Hyman," by Katrin Hyman, pp. 275–278.
Also includes "The Caldecott Spectrum," by Barbara Bader, pp. 279–314, critical analysis with illustrations from the books, and "A Decade of Books: A Critic's Response," by Ethel L. Heins, pp. 323–342, includes critical comments on picture books, pp. 325–333.

278. _____. *The Illustrator's Notebook*. Boston: Horn Book, 1978. 153pp.

Profusely illustrated in b & w and color. All articles are excerpted from *Horn Book Magazine* or another of their publications. They cover many aspects of the field, but especially for children.

Part I, "Notes on the History and Philosophy of Illustration, Its Standards, and Its Place in the Arts," pp. 1–28, includes the views of Fritz Eichenberg, Lynd Ward, Warren Chappell, Hilda van Stockum, Barbara Cooney, Marcia Brown, Leonard Weisgard and Lee Kingman.

Part II, "Notes about Artists and by Artists about Their Work," pp. 29–78, includes Marcia Brown, Ernest H. Shepard, Dahlov Ipcar and editor Grace Allen Hogarth talking about their own work; Dudley Lunt on N.C. Wyeth; Hilda van Stockum on Randolph Caldecott; Rose Dobbs on Wanda Gag; and a series of "Artists's Choice" pages where artists choose the work of another for comment.

Part III, "Notes about Illustration and Techniques," pp. 79–122, has general notes by Lynd Ward and Walter Lorraine and specific descriptions of techniques by Leonard Weisgard, Ezra Jack Keats, Evaline Ness, Blair Lent, Adrienne Adams, Juliet Kepes, Dahlov Ipcar, Lynd Ward, Barbara Cooney, Ed Emberly and Edwin Tunis.

Part IV, "Notes about Illustration as Communication," pp. 123–142, contains articles by Lynd Ward, Joseph Low, Bettina Ehrlich, Uri Shulevitz, Blair Lent and Gerald McDermott.

279. Kirkpatrick, D.L., ed. *Twentieth-Century Children's Writers*. New York: St. Martin's, 1978. 1507pp.

No illustrations. The scope is those writers published after 1900. Appendix includes some late 19th century. Includes some illustrators; e.g., Anglund, Ardizzone, Bemelmans, Brooke, D'Aulaire, etc. Gives basic biographical facts, a list of their publications, sometimes a quotation from the artist about the work, and one or two paragraphs of criticism. Section on books in translation.

The second edition (1983) is basically the same book with some names added and others omitted. For example, Ahlberg is added, Anglund omitted. Information on specific people seems the same, but both need to be checked for particular persons.

* Klemin, Diana. *The Art of Art for Children's Books*. Cited above as item 177.

280. Kujoth, Jean Spealman. *Best-Selling Children's Books*. Metuchen, New Jersey: Scarecrow, 1973. 305pp.

Sixty-eight publishers were surveyed to find the names of children's books that had sold more that 100,000 copies. The list by author includes a brief description. Chapter Four, pp. 192–220, lists the best-sellers by illustrator. In chapter seven the books are grouped by "type of book, subject category and age level" and those for preschool—grade 3 are considered picture books and can be isolated this way.

281. Kuskin, Karla. "Two Illustrators Can Be Better than One." *New York Times Book Review* (January 6, 1985): 24.

Descriptions of the works of five married couples (Provensens, Dillons, Berenstains, Lobels, Dewey and Aruego), pointing out styles of working.

* Lanes, Selma. *Down the Rabbit Hole: Adventures and Misadventures in the Realm of Children's Literature.* Cited above as item 181.

* Lemieux, Louise. *Pleins Feux Sur la Litterature de Jeunesse au Canada Français.* Cited above as item 184.

* Lewis, John. *The Twentieth Century Book.* Cited above as item 37.

* *Lively Art of Picture Books.* Cited above as item 190.

* Mahony, Bertha E., et al. *Illustrators of Children's Books, 1744–1945.* Cited above as item 41.

* Mahony, Bertha E., and Elinor Whitney. *Contemporary Illustrators of Children's Books.* Cited above as item 42.

282. Meyer, Susan E. *America's Great Illustrators.* New York: Abrams, 1978. 311pp.

    Profusely illustrated in b & w and color. Introduction, pp. 8–37, presents historic background and technical processes. Among the illustrators whose lives and art are discussed are Howard Pyle, pp. 40–63, and N.C. Wyeth, pp. 64–87.

* _____. *A Treasury of the Great Children's Book Illustrators.* Cited above as item 45.

283. Miller, Bertha Mahony, and Elinor Whitney Field, eds. *Caldecott Medal Books: 1938–1957.* With acceptance papers, biographies and related materials chiefly from the *Horn Book Magazine.* Boston: Horn Book, 1957. 329pp.

    Some b & w illustrations. A year-by-year compilation with both acceptance and biographical papers. See Kingman, Lee, ed. *Newbery and Caldecott Medal Books: 1956–1965, 1965–1975* for subsequent years.

* _____, et al., compilers. *Illustrators of Children's Books, 1946–1956.* Cited above as item 197.

284. Ovenden, Graham, ed. *The Illustrators of* Alice in Wonderland *and* Through the Looking Glass. New York: St. Martin's, 1972. 88pp.

Introduction by John Davis, pp. 7–14, discusses Carroll and Tenniel. Lists many of the artists who have illustrated *Alice* since, with brief comments on their work. Pages 8–98 are mainly b & w illustrations, chapter by chapter.

285. Peppin, Brigid, and Lucy Micklethwait. *Dictionary of British Illustrators: The Twentieth Century.* London: John Murray, 1983. 336pp.

Neatly organized, concise biographies of almost 1000 illustrators published between 1900 and 1975 in Britain. Includes many titles of books illustrated, periodicals in which work appears, sources of information, and, in about a third of the cases, a b & w reproduction.

* *Picture Book Design Conference: From Conception to Consumption.* Cited above as item 205.

286. Pitz, Henry C. *The Brandywine Tradition.* Boston: Houghton Mifflin, 1968. 252pp.

Sixteen color and 32 b & w plates, some of which are children's book illustrations. A description of the Brandywine area and its history; of the artists who have worked or currently work there. Those who illustrated children's books include Howard Pyle, pp. 33–162; Jesse Wilcox Smith, pp. 98 and 179; and N.C. Wyeth, pp. 188–208.

* Poltarnees, Welleran. *All Mirrors Are Magic Mirrors: Reflections On Pictures Found In Children's Books.* Cited above as item 56.

287. *Profiles in Literature.* (Videotape.) Norristown, Pennsylvania:
      Dr. Jaqueline Weiss, dates vary. 3/4 inch U-Matic, 1/2 inch
      VHS. 30 minutes each.

      Interviews with authors, illustrators and editors of children's
      books. Those concerned with picture books include #4, Stan, Jan
      and Michael Berenstain (color) 1979; #10, Marguerite de Angeli
      (color) 1976; #11, Tomie de Paola (color), 1984; #13, Tom and
      Muriel Feelings (b & w) 1971; #21, Tana Hoban and Susan
      Hirschman (b & w) 1975; #24, Ezra Jack Keats (b & w) 1970;
      #27, Joe and Beth Krush (b & w) 1972; #32, Arnold Lobel (b &
      w) 1973; #33, Robert McCloskey (b & w) 1977; #43, Maurice
      Sendak (color) 1977; #45, John Steptoe (b & w) 1975; #50, Lynd
      Ward and May McNeer (b & w) 1974.

*   Reed, Walt, and Roger Reed. *The Illustrator in America, 1880–
      1980: A Century of Illustration.* Cited above as item 58.

288. Robinson, Moira, ed. *Readings in Children's Literature:
      Proceeding of the National Seminar on Children's Literature.*
      Victoria, Australia: Frankston State College, 1975. 293pp.

      Includes "A Dialogue on Illustrating," pp. 104–123, in which
      John Burningham and Helen Oxenbury both talk about their
      books and illustrations.

289. Roginski, James W. *Behind the Covers: Interviews with
      Authors and Illustrators of Books for Children and Young
      Adults.* Littleton, Colorado: Libraries Unlimited, 1985. 249pp.

      Includes Martha Alexander, pp. 1–7; Donald Crews, pp. 42–50;
      Demi (Charlotte Dumaresq Hunt), pp. 59–72; Charles
      Mikolaycak, pp. 138–153; Rolf Myller, pp. 154–160; Elise
      Primavera, pp. 161–166; Ellen Raskin, pp. 167–176. Roginski
      includes a biographical note and a prelude, in which he describes
      the subject and his impressions of how and where he or she
      works. A bibliography of the subjects' works, a list of awards
      won, and possessers of further information follow.

Appendices include the library collections where original art and/or manuscripts are retained, an explanation of the awards and honors won, and bibliographies of sources.

290. _____. *Newbery and Caldecott Medalists and Honor Book Winners: Bibliographies and Resource Materials through 1977.* Littleton, Colorado: Libraries Unlimited, 1982. 339pp.

For each entry lists awards won, books written and/or illustrated, what media presentations have been made, the collections where the original manuscripts, art work and non-book materials by that person are, what exhibitions of art work have been held, and a list of books for background reading.

* Ryder, John. *Artists of a Certain Line: A Selection of Illustrators for Children's Books.* Cited above as item 217.

291. Sarkissian, Adele, ed. *Something About the Author Autobiography Series.* Detroit: Gale, 1986. Volume 1, 1986.

Several b & w photographs illustrate each article. Authors relate varying amounts of information on their life and work. A complete listing of each author's works and an index to publishers, geographic references, personal names and titles are included. How many authors who are also illustrators to be included is not clear.

Volume One contains Leonard Everett Fisher, Nonny Hogrogian, Evaline Ness, and Rosemary Wells.

292. Selden, Rebecca, and Sarah Smedman. "The Art of the Contemporary Picture Book." *Proceedings of the Seventh Annual Conference of the Children's Literature Association.* Baylor University (March, 1980): 152–165.

Examines artists who illustrate in a wide variety of styles, including Sendak, Steig, Lent, Lionni, Ward, McDermott, Lawrence, Girfalconi, Wildsmith, Macaulay and Burkert, with a bit about each of them and their art. References are made to page numbers of examples shown in slides but not pictured.

293. Senick, Gerard J., ed. *Children's Literature Review: Excerpts from Reviews, Criticism and Commentary on Books for Children and Young People.* Detroit: Gale, 1976 (ongoing).

Each volume includes numerous b & w illustrations from books and portraits of the authors and author-illustrators covered. These are listed alphabetically, followed by a biocritical introduction, comments by the subject if available, list of works chronologically with excerpts from several reviews, and bibliographic citation. Illustrators are not listed in a separate index, but each volume has a cumulative author, title and, since volume six, a nationality index. Volume 12 (1987) includes many illustrators in its cumulative author index. Since volume five, guest essays cover special topics.

294. Smaridge, Norah. *Famous Author-Illustrators for Young People.* New York: Dodd, Mead, 1973. 159pp.

Illustrated with b & w photographs or drawings of the illustrators. Includes biographical information and some criticism of: Edward Lear, pp. 11–18; Kate Greenaway, pp. 19–28; Beatrix Potter, pp. 29–36; Robert Lawson, pp. 37–43; Wanda Gag, pp. 44–53; Lois Lenski, pp. 54–61; Marie Hall Ets, pp. 62–69; Ludwig Bemelmans, pp. 70–77; H.A. Rey, pp. 78–84; Roger Duvoisin, pp. 85–92; Theodor Geisel (Dr. Seuss), pp. 93–100; Leo Lionni, pp. 101–106; Robert McCloskey, pp. 106–112; Brinton Turkel, pp. 113–117; Marcia Brown, pp. 118–123; Richard Scarry, pp. 124–129; Joan Walsh Anglund, pp. 130–137; Maurice Sendak, pp. 138–145; Tomi Ungerer, pp. 146–152.

* Targ, William, ed. *Bibliophile in the Nursery: A Bookman's Treasury of Collectors Lore on Old and Rare Children's Books.* Cited above as item 63.

295. Ward, Martha Eads. *Illustrators of Books for Young People.* New York: Scarecrow, 1970. 166pp.

Contains 370 brief, one-paragraph biographies.

296. _____. *Illustrators of Books for Young People.* 2nd ed. New York: Scarecrow, 1975. 223pp.

Contains 750 brief paragraphs of biographies. Both the 1st and 2nd editions include Caldecott winners, title index and references to other sources.

297. Wintle, Justin, and Emma Fisher. *The Pied Pipers: Interviews with the Influential Creators of Children's Literature.* New York: Paddington Press Ltd., Two Continents Publishing Group, 1974. 320pp.

Some b & w illustrations and photographs of subjects. Introduction, pp. 11–19, gives history of children's book publishing, including current assessment. Individual interviews with brief biographical and critical comments followed by question-and-answer format on life and work. Artists include Maurice Sendak, pp. 20–23; Edward Ardizzone, pp. 35–48; Charles Keeping, pp. 49–63; Richard Scarry, pp. 64–76; Laurent de Brunhoff, pp. 77–86; Dr. Seuss (letter, answers) pp. 113–123.

298. Woolman, Bertha. *The Caldecott Award: The Winners and the Honor Books.* New rev. ed. Minneapolis: T.S. Denison, 1981. 96pp.

An explanation of the award; questions and answers about the winners and honor books for children of various ages. List of the illustrators with some information about them, pp. 29–50. Award winners listed pp. 51–56. General sources for further information pp. 57–58. Sources on each individual artist are listed, pp. 59–94.

PART V

Books, Articles, and Audiovisual Materials on Individual Picture Book Artists

299. Abrahamson, Richard F., and Marilyn Colvin. "Tomie de Paola: Children's Choice." *Reading Teacher* 33 (December, 1979): 264–269.

    Includes discussion of his treatment of costumes and borders in *Clown of God*, comparisons with works by others, illustrations in *When Everyone Was Fast Asleep* and follow-up activities for children.

300. Agree, Rose. "Lionni's Artichokes: An Interview." *Wilson Library Bulletin* 44, no. 9 (May, 1970): 947–950.

    His books as his "autobiography" and his illustrations as stage sets are among the ideas expressed as Lionni answers questions about his work.
    Also in Mary Lou White, *Children's Literature: Criticism and Response* (item 244, above).

 * Alderson, Brian. *Sing a Song for Sixpence: The English Picture Book Tradition and Randolph Caldecott.* Cited above as item 2.

301. Ammon, Richard. "Profile: David Macaulay." *Language Arts* 59 (April, 1982): 374–378.

An appreciative description of him, where he lives and works and his life, with quotations. Notes on some of his books and the art within them. B & w portrait photos and small illustrations.

302. Anderson, Dennis. "Tomie de Paola, Tough and Tender Storyteller." *Instructor* 89, no. 8 (March, 1980): 32–34, 38.

Interview includes his feelings about children and the children's book world. Nothing about his illustration.

303. Andersen, Han Christian, and Kate Greenaway. *Kate Greenaway's Original Drawings for the Snow Queen.* New York: Schocken, 1981. 58pp.

Studies from an unpublished edition. "Afterword," pp. 53–58, has comments on the author and the artist by Michael Patrick Hearn.

304. Aoki, Hisako. "A Conversation with Mitsumasa Anno." *Horn Book* 59, no. 2 (April, 1983): 137–145.

Anno's views on art from his perspective as a former art teacher. Background of some of his works, notes on how he works.

305. Ardizzone, Edward. "Creation of a Picture Book." *Top of the News* (December, 1959): 289–298.

Discusses his problems with text and illustrations in creating *Little Tim and the Brave Sea Captain.* Gives examples of how he progressed and the choices made.

306. *Arnold Lobel.* (Sound Filmstrip.) Random House/Miller Brody.

Lobel introduces himself and tells about his life and work.

307. *Beatrix Potter Had a Pet Named Peter.* (Sound Filmstrip.) Westminster, Maryland: Random House/Miller Brody, 1985. One filmstrip, one cassette. Also available transferred to videotape, 14 minutes.

The story of her life and her creation of Peter Rabbit.

308. Bechtel, Louise S. "Boris Artzybasheff." *Horn Book* 42 (April, 1966): 176–180.

An appreciation, including information on his life and discussion of the art of his illustration in many of his books.

309. *Bill Peet in His Studio.* (Videotape.) Boston: Houghton Mifflin, no date. 3/4 inch, 1/2 inch Beta, 1/2 inch VHS. 13 minutes.

Peet tells of his early days and his work with Disney studios. He demonstrates how his characters and stories develop as he sketches. Finally, he talks about his appearances in schools and the many letters and pictures he gets from children.

310. Blake, Quentin. "Wild Washerwomen, Hired Sportsmen, and Enormous Crocodiles." *Horn Book* 57 (October, 1981): 505–513.

His account of how he works to "act the story" when he collaborates, plus how he draws. His own books start as pictures or series of pictures. Discusses some individual books. B & w examples.

311. Blegvad, Erik. *Self-Portrait: Erik Blegvad.* Reading, Massachusetts: Addison-Wesley, 1979. 32pp.

Profusely illustrated in color by the author and others. Beginning with other members of his family with drawing talent, Blegvad tells of his childhood in Denmark, his study of art and the start of his career, with examples.

* Brown, Marcia. *Lotus Seeds: Children, Pictures and Books.* Cited above as item 109.

312. Burkert, Nancy Ekholm. "A Second Look: *Lion.*" *Horn Book* 56 (December, 1980): 671–676.

An affectionate appreciation of this classic, with analysis of the design and the art work of the illustrator, including details of his technique using Dinobase for the effect of a lithograph. Comparison of the original with the smaller, less effective paperback.

313. _____. *The Art of Nancy Ekholm Burkert*. Edited by David Larkin. Introduced by Michael Danoff. New York: Harper and Row, 1977. Unpaginated.

Forty illustrations in color, others are in b & w. A few pages of her life, some quotations about herself, some analysis of her art, plus examples of the children's book illustrations and a few other paintings.

314. Burton, Virginia Lee. "Making Picture Books." *Horn Book* 19 (July–August, 1943): 228–229.

Her brief discussion of how she works, particulary on *The Little House*.

315. Cech, John. "Maurice Sendak: Off the Page." *Horn Book* 62, no. 3 (May–June, 1986): 305–313.

Describes some of the processes involved in creating operas of several of Sendak's books; mainly, *Where the Wild Things Are*, as well as his setting of *The Nutcracker* ballet.

316. *Children of the Northern Lights*. (16mm color film.) (Videocassette.) Weston, Connecticut: Weston Woods. No date. 20 min.

Ingri and Edgar Parin D'Aulaire discuss their work and describe their lithographic process of illustrating. Includes scenes from the animations made from their books.

317. Conrad, Barnaby III. "Maurice Sendak." *Horizon* 24, no. 5 (May, 1981): 24–33.

A lush, colorful tribute.

318. Cornell, Robert W. "Robert Lawson: For All Children." *Elementary English* 50 (May, 1973): 718–725, 738.

   An appreciation detailing his life and each book he did, with some quotes. Little analysis of his art.

319. Cott, Jonathan. "Maurice Sendak, King of All Wild Things." *Rolling Stone*, no. 229 (Dec. 30, 1976): 48–59.

   An extensive and lively interview at the artist's house. Wide-ranging in subject matter and uninhibited in its conversation.

320. Crichton, Jennifer. "Dr. Seuss Turns 80." *Publishers Weekly* (February 10, 1984): 22–23.

   Summary of other works, plus longer discussion of *Butter Battle Book*. Interview with quotes.

 * Darling, Harold, and Peter Neumeyer, eds. *Image and Maker: An Annual Dedicated to the Consideration of Book Illustration.* Cited above as item 131.

321. *David Macaulay in his Studio.* (Videotape.) Boston: Houghton Mifflin, no date. 3/4 inch, 1/2 inch Beta, 1/2 inch VHS. 25 minutes.

   After telling something about how he became an illustrator, Macaulay shows us where and how he works, describing in particular the gathering of the background information and the progression from first drawing to finished and printed volume of his book *Pyramid.*

322. Davis, Mary Gould. *Randolph Caldecott, 1846–1886: An Appreciation.* Philadelphia: Lippincott, 1946. 47pp.

   Part I, pp. 1–22, "The picture books," has a description and some children's reactions. Part II, pp. 25–44, "The artist," discusses his life and art. Bibliography includes his books and books about him.

323. de Angeli, Marguerite. *Butter at the Old Price: The Autobiography of Marguerite de Angeli.* New York: Doubleday, 1971. 258pp.

Illustrated with b & w photographs, drawings, and a seven-page insert that includes color reproductions. Along with the details of her life, de Angeli gives us her first memories of her father and his artwork. But it was not until after her brief singing career, marriage, and the birth of three children that she followed an inclination and went to art school. After 14 years of illustrating, she began to write her own books. Brief discussion of her technique, but many details on her life and family.

324. *Dr. Seuss from Then to Now.* New York: Random House, 1987. 96pp.

Over 250 illustrations in b & w and color fill this catalog compiled by the San Diego Museum of Art to accompany the exhibit celebrating 60 years of Dr. Seuss.

325. Durrell, Ann. "Nonny Hogrogian." *Library Journal* 91 (March 15, 1966), also *School Library Journal* 13 (March, 1966): 128–129.

Some notes on how Hogrogian works.

326. *Edward Ardizzone.* (16mm color film.) (Videocassette.) Weston: Weston Woods, no date. 13 min.

The artist live, discussing his life and work in his studio in Kent, England, and talking with children. Includes some of his sketches.

327. Edwards, James P. *Randolph Caldecott.* ERIC Document ED 196020, 1980. 18pp.

Summary of the facts of his life with a description of his work and changes in style.

328. Elzea, Rowland. *Howard Pyle.* New York: Peacock/Bantam, 1975. Unpaginated.

Chiefly a portfolio of 43 of his color illustrations. Rowland's five-page introduction to the illustrations covers Pyle's life and the milieu in which he worked. Some critical comments included.

329. Engen, Rodney. *Kate Greenaway: A Biography.* New York: Schocken Books, 1981. 240pp.

Many b & w and color illustrations, including photographs. Covers her childhood, education, art school training, beginnings as greeting card illustrator, her meetings with Caldecott, Ruskin, her success, her fall from favor and its recovery after her death. Some analysis of the influences on her work and a little about her style. Lists all her illustrated books.

* *Evolution of a Graphic Concept: The Stonecutter.* Cited above as item 76.

330. *Ezra Jack Keats.* (16 mm film.) Weston, Connecticut: Weston Woods, no date. 17min.

In his studio the late artist talks about his life and work. Includes adaptation of *A Letter to Amy* to show how he works.

331. Feelings, Tom. "The Artist at Work: Technique and the Artist's Vision." *Horn Book* 61, no. 6 (November–December, 1985): 685–695.

Relates his life experiences as they have influenced his work as a Black American artist. Details how he works in general and also on particular books. Five b & w examples.

332. "Frasconi's Brio With a Book." *Horizon* 3 (March, 1961): 122–128.

Brief introduction to his life and work, with description and a photo of his one-of-a-kind books. Several b & w and color prints reproduced.

333. Frith, Margaret. "Interview with Eric Hill." *Horn Book* 63, no. 5 (September/October, 1987): 577–585.

His background, how he came to do the books about Spot for his young son, where his ideas come from, how he does his art work and works out his stories.

334. Gag, Wanda. *Growing Pains: Diaries and Drawings for the Years 1908–1917*. New York: Coward-McCann, 1940. 479pp.

Sixty b & w reproductions of her "fine art" work as well as her illustrations. Gives account in her own words of her time in school studying art.

* *Gail E. Haley: Wood and Linoleum Illustration.* (Sound Filmstrip.) Cited above as item 77.

335. Golynets, Sergei. *Ivan Bilibin.* New York: Harry N. Abrams, 1981. 226pp.

Chiefly 195 illustrations including 98 full color plates and some b & w photographs. A critical summary of his artwork and his place in the Art Nouveau movement, pp. 5–22, of his life with chronology and quotes from his letters, pp. 181–208. His book illustrations are not separated from his work in general.

336. Gormsen, J. "Interview With Svend Otto S. The Famous Danish Illustrator." *Bookbird* 17, no. 1 (1979): 6–12.

He briefly describes his life and early training and discusses his current work, influences and aims.

337. Green, Roger Lancelyn, ed. *Lewis Carroll by Roger Lancelyn Green; E. Nesbit by Anthea Bell; Howard Pyle by Elizabeth Nesbit.* London: Bodley Head, 1968. 219pp.

The section on Pyle, pp. 163–219, discusses his life and his "theories of illustration," pp. 178–188. Notes on his technique and the effect of new photo-engraving methods on it. Stresses in particular the results of his teaching: how he was an inspiration and challenge to his students without imitation.

338. Greenaway, Kate. *Kate Greenaway.* New York: Rizzoli, 1977. 49pp.

Chiefly colored illustrations. Short text about Greenaway accompanies reproductions of her work from the Victoria and Albert Museum originally printed by woodblock process by Evans.

339. Hamilton, Lawrie. "The Art in Lois Lenski's Book *The Little Auto.*" *The Barnes Foundation Journal of the Art Department* 4, no. 2 (Autumn, 1973): 53–63.

Discusses the words of the story and the illustrations as they relate to design and other theories of art and "fine" artists, espoused by the Barnes Foundation.

340. Harris, Muriel. "Impressions of Sendak." *Elementary English* 48, no. 7 (November, 1971): 825–832.

An interview with the artist when he still lived in a "fortress against any of today's distractions" in New York City. Includes his comments on his family and early years and notes on some sources of inspiration. Some brief pictorial analysis of *In the Night Kitchen.*

341. Hearn, Michael Patrick. "Drawing Out William Steig." *Bookbird* 3–4 (1982): 61–65.

Steig talks briefly about his background, how he came to children's books, and how he works, including why he uses animal characters.

342.   _____. "Maurice Boutet de Monvel: Master of the French
        Picture Book." *Horn Book* 55 (April, 1979): 170–181.

        Covers his life, training, and how he came to illustrate for
        children, plus possible influences on his work. Some of his own
        comments are quoted. Analysis of some of his books and
        suggestions of his influence on picture book artists today.

343.   _____. "The 'Ubiquitous' Trina Schart Hyman." *American
        Artist* 43 (May, 1979): 36–43, 96–97.

        Many b & w and color examples of her illustrations. Describes
        her life, her art training, her early illustrations, and her
        controversy-provoking ones. Notes on her work with *Cricket*
        magazine. Detailed analysis of her techniques and method of
        character development, appreciation of her "drama."

344.   _____. "W.W. Denslow: The Forgotten Illustrator." *American
        Artist* 37 (May, 1973): 40–45, 71–73.

        B & w and color illustrations. Summary of his career and work.
        Description of techniques used. Some quotations from his writing
        about himself.

345.   Hepler, Susan Ingrid. "Profile: Tomie de Paola: A Gift to
        Children." *Language Arts* 56 (March, 1979): 296–301.

        Summary of his life; some quotations on life and work. Notes
        on story and art work of many books. B & w photo portrait.

346.   Higgins, James. "William Steig: Champion for Romance."
        Children's Literature in Education 9, no. 1 (Spring, 1978): 3–16.

        An appreciation of Steig's fiction, not his illustrations. Pages
        10–15 are from a "conversation" between Higgins and Steig which
        covers how he came to write for children, his feelings about it,
        and a few sentences on his illustrations. One b & w illustration.

347. Hoare, Geoffrey. "The Work of David Macaulay." *Children's Literature in Education* 8, no. 1 (Spring, 1977): 12–20.

> Many b & w illustrations. Notes on children's changing preferences in illustration, perhaps because of media exposure as Hoare analyzes Macaulay's art. Criticism of his inability to draw believable figures, his "Vaguenesses," other lacks of connections between illustrations and missing specifics. Provocative discussion.

348. Holme, Bryan. *The Kate Greenaway Book.* New York: Studio Viking, 1976. (Penguin, 1977.) 144pp.

> Profusely illustrated in alternating b & w and color two-page spreads. "Success," pp. 7–11, comments on her impact on her time. "Background," pp. 13–32, gives introductory biographical information. Selections from her works follow, each preceded by background information and contemporary criticism. Their arrangement is more or less chronological.

* *How a Picture Book is Made: The Making of the Island of the Skog from Conception to Finished Book.* Cited above as item 84.

349. Hudson, Derek. *Arthur Rackham: His Life and Work.* New York: Scribner's, 1960. 180pp.

> Some b & w illustrations and many tipped-in color plates. A chronological review of his life and work, with critical comments by the author. Some quotations from Rackham and his contemporaries about his art. Appendices include the author's sources and checklist of the printed work of Rackham.

350. Hurley, Beatrice J. "Wanda Gag—Artist, Author." *Elementary English* 32 (October, 1955): 347–354.

> Summary of her early family life and growth, and quotations from her biography, *Growing Pains* (New York: Coward-McCann, 1940). Notes on some books, but no analysis of pictures.

351. Hutton, Warwick. "How Jonah and the Great Fish Began." *Horn Book* 61, no.1 (January/ February, 1985): 35–37.

   In this speech written on receipt of the Boston Globe–Horn Book Award for illustration, Hutton describes how he decided to do the book and his technique for the illustrations.

352. Hyman, Trina Schart. *Self-Portrait: Trina Schart Hyman.* Reading, Massachusetts: Addison-Wesley, 1981. 32pp.

   The simple story of how she grew up and became an illustrator, rich with details of her friends and life.

353. Irvine, Ruth R. "Marie Hall Ets—Her Picture Story Books." *Elementary English* 33 (May, 1956): 259–265.

   B & w photo portrait, few b & w illustrations. Summary of some of her books as to story, with only brief comments on the illustrations.

354. *James Daugherty.* (16mm color film.) (Videocassette.) Weston, Connecticut: Weston Woods, no date. 19 min.

   Interview at his home and studio where he discusses his work as illustrator as well as author and historian.

355. Jones, Helen L. *Robert Lawson, Illustrator: A Selection of His Characteristic Illustrations.* Boston: Little Brown, 1972. 121pp.

   The illustrations are divided into types and briefly introduced. "Vital statistics and techniques" fill pp. 109–114. A list of books illustrated by Robert Lawson is on pp. 119–120.

356. Keeping, Charles. "My Work as a Children's Illustrator." *Children's Literature Association Quarterly* 8, no. 4 (Winter, 1983): 14–19.

   His background, childhood memories, art school training and start as an illustrator. He tells how he began to write for children, and the background of some of his other books, including discussion of his controversial titles.

357. Kingman, Lee. "Virginia Lee Burton's Dynamic Sense of Design." *Horn Book* 46 (October–December, 1970): 449–460, 593–602.

A detailed analysis of her illustrations and technique in *Calico the Wonder Horse* is included in this appreciation of Burton, along with some information on her life, background and training, and five b & w illustrations.

358. Klingberg, Delores R. "Profile: Eric Carle." *Language Arts* 54 (April, 1977): 445–452.

B & w photo portrait and examples of his original art. The facts on his life and training and his concerns, plus notes on his collage technique come from him. A description, book-by-book, by Klingberg of his works.

359. Knox, Rawle. *The Work of E.H. Shepard.* New York: Schocken, 1979. 256pp.

Profusely illustrated in b & w and color. The story of Shepard's life, his start as an artist and the many illustrations he did besides his work for children are detailed. Chapter eight, "A Master of Line" by Bevis Hillier, pp. 246–251, is an appreciation of his skill.

360. Kroll, Steven. "Steig: Nobody is Grown-up." *New York Times Book Review* (June 28, 1987): 26.

In this interview, Steig talks briefly about how he illustrates, along with comments on his work and life.

361. Lacy, Lyn. *Randolph Caldecott, the Man Behind the Medal.* (Sound Filmstrip.) Weston, Connecticut: Weston Woods, 1983. 1 filmstrip, 1 cassette. 57 frames, 15 min.

Covers his life and art, including his drawing and illustrations for picture books. Also some information on the medal.

362. Lahr, John. "The Playful Art of Maurice Sendak." *New York Times Magazine* (October 12, 1980): 44–48, 52–60.

A perceptive exploration of the artist's development, and the interrelationship of his books and his theatrical designs.

363. Landes, Sonia. *A Closer Look at Peter Rabbit.* (Sound Filmstrip.) Weston, Connecticut: Weston Woods, 1984. 1 Filmstrip, 1 Cassette. 49 frames, 17 min.

Analysis of words and pictures and how they work together. Comparison with another, less effective illustrator.

364. Lanes, Selma G. "A Second Look: Joan of Arc." *Horn Book* 58 (February, 1982): 79–83.

A short background introduction and brief criticism of text, but mainly a detailed analysis of the illustrations and their art, with consideration of the overall design as well.

365. ———. *The Art of Maurice Sendak.* New York: Harry N. Abrams, 1980. 278pp.

Profusely illustrated in b & w and 94 in full color. Includes photographs. Both biography and discussion of works. Conversations with him included.

366. ———. "Ezra Jack Keats: In Memoriam." *Horn Book* 40 (September/October, 1984): 551–558.

Includes personal reminiscences, quotations from the artist and those who knew him about his life and work, and an appreciation of his art.

367. Larkin, David, ed. *The Art of Nancy Ekholm Burkert.* New York: Harper and Row, 1977. Unpaginated.

Chiefly illustrations, mostly in color. Basically a portfolio of her artwork only, some of which is book illustration. An eight-page introduction by Michael Danoff details her life and analyzes her art technique. He also includes quotations on her life and work.

368. _____. *The Fantastic Paintings of Charles and William Heath Robinson.* New York: Bantam, 1976. Unpaginated.

Chiefly 40 full-page color plates of the illustrators. A brief introduction covers their life, some discussion of their art and a few quotations from the artists.

369. *Laurent de Brunhoff, Daydreamer.* (Sound Filmstrip.) Westminster, Maryland: Random House, 1982. 1 Filmstrip, 1 Cassette.

Interview. Tells how he works.

370. Lent, Blair. "Artist at Work: Cardboard Cuts." *Horn Book* 41 (August, 1965): 408–412.

A factual step-by-step account of how he makes cardboard cuts, including specifics on the art in some of his books, with b & w examples.

371. Linder, Leslie. *History of the Tale of Peter Rabbit.* New York: Warne, 1977. 64pp.

From its origin in an illustrated letter through writing, editing and publication, with related correspondence.

372. _____, and Enid Linder. *The Art of Beatrix Potter.* New York: Warne, 1955. 406pp.

Detailed analysis of development of art through her life. Profusely illustrated.

373. Lobel, Arnold. "Birthdays and Beginnings." *Theory Into Practice* 21, no. 4 (Fall, 1982): 322–324.

Remarks at the Children's Literature Conference at the Ohio State University in January, 1982, on a day that happened also to be his birthday. Some remarks on his childhood and how his distance from it makes it harder to write for children. After inspiration from Lear and Grandville, how he began to write *Pigericks*, and a bit on how he does his drawing: "the dessert after the spinach of writing."

374. Lorraine, Walter. "An Interview with Maurice Sendak." *Wilson Library Bulletin* 52 (October, 1977): 326–336.

Sendak discusses his interpretive illustrations of Grimm's and other tales, his techniques, and gives his definitions of "picture book." Mentions that he is not happy with the conservatism of publishers nor with contemporary criticism.

375. *The Man Who Invented Snoopy.* (Sound Filmstrip.) Westminster, Maryland: Random House, 1982. 1 Filmstrip, 1 Cassette.

Charles Schulz discusses his life and work.

376. Marantz, Sylvia, and Kenneth Marantz. "Interview with Ann Jonas." *Horn Book* 63, no. 3 (May–June, 1987): 308–313.

How she works, with details on some particular books. B & w illustrations.

377. ———. "An Interview with Anthony Browne." *Horn Book* 61, no. 6 (November–December, 1985): 696–704.

How he became an illustrator, how he works, thoughts on some of his books. B & w examples from *Gorilla* and *Hansel and Gretel*.

378. ———. "Interview with Paul O. Zelinsky." *Horn Book* 62, no. 3 (May–June, 1986): 295–304.

Discusses how he came to illustration, how he attacks each book, with some details on *Hansel and Gretel*. B & w examples.

379. _____. "M.B. Goffstein: An Interview." *Horn Book* 62, no. 6 (November–December, 1986): 688–694.

How the artist works, with some details on individual books. Three b & w examples.

380. *Maurice Sendak—1965*. (16mm color film.) (Videocassette.) Weston, Connecticut: Weston Woods, 1965. 14 min.

Interview in his New York apartment. He discusses his early books, influence of painters and composers, and *Where the Wild Things Are*.

381. May, Jill P., ed. "Howard Pyle Commemorative." *Children's Literature Association Quarterly* 8, no. 2 (Summer, 1983): 9–34.

Includes Patricia Dooley, "Romance and Realism: Pyle's Book Illustrations for Children," pp. 17–19, a discussion of his "decoration" style in many of his books, both the design and the individual details of the illustrations.

382. _____. "Illustration as Interpretation: Trina Hyman's Folk Tales." *Children's Literature Association Quarterly* 10 (Fall, 1985): 127–131.

Discusses Hyman's version of *Snow White, Rapunzel* and *Little Red Riding Hood* in great detail, including influences, models for the characters, symbolism, book and page design, clothing of characters, and parallels with Hyman's life, quoting Hyman as well.

383. _____. "Trina S. Hyman." *Children's Literature Association Quarterly* 11, no. 1 (Spring, 1986): 44.

Interview that emphasizes the artist "with a strong understanding of art, of psychology, and of people—including children." Illustration as interpretation.

384. McKee, Barbara. "Van Allsburg: From a Different Perspective." *Horn Book* 65, no. 5 (September–October, 1986): 566–571.

A detailed analysis of the artwork in each of Van Allsburg's first six books, showing how his drawing of figures evolved with the development of his addition of color. Also discusses his increasing psychological depth of character. B & w examples.

385. McPherson, William. "Maurice Sendak in Profile." *Washington Post Book World* (May 10, 1981): 1, 8–9, 12.

A thoughtful interview and appreciation of a variety of the artist's works.

386. McWhorter, George. "Arthur Rackham: The Search Goes On." *Horn Book* 48 (February, 1972): 82–87.

A brief appreciation of his development as an illustrator, as part of a discussion of the continuing rise in the price of his original works and the consequent search for more.

387. *Meet Stan and Jan Berenstain.* (Sound filmstrip.) Westminster, Maryland: Random House, 1982. 1 Filmstrip, 1 Cassette.

The Berenstains tell how they work together and both write and illustrate their books.

388. Mercier, Jean F. "Sendak on Sendak." *Publishers Weekly* (April 10, 1981): 45–46.

Some small b & w illustration. A detailed description by the author of the development of *Outside Over Time*, including the relevance to his own childhood.

389. Meyer, S. "N.C. Wyeth." *American Artist* 39 (February, 1975): 38–45, 94–100.

B & w and color examples of his illustrations, portrait. His life and work, quotations from his writing, description of how he painted. His influence on his children and other artists.

390. Michel, Joan Hess. "A Visit with Tomi Ungerer." *American Artist* 33 (May, 1969): 40–45, 78–79.

Many illustrations. Informal description of the artist, his work place, his life and some of his books for both children and adults. Some analysis of his art.

391. Mikolaycak, Charles. "The Artist at Work: The Challenge of the Picture Book." *Horn Book* 62 (March, 1986): 167–173.

A detailed description of how this artist works and his ideas about how picture books should be illustrated.

392. *Mr. Shepard and Mr. Milne.* (16mm color film.) (Videocassette.) Weston, Connecticut: Weston Woods, no date. 29 min.

The original Christopher Robin discusses the collaboration of the author and illustrator. Includes visits to original locales.

393. Ness, Evaline. "The Artist at Work: Woodcut Illustration." *Horn Book* 40 (October, 1964): 520–522.

A detailed and loving account of how she makes woodcuts.

394. Painter, Helen W. "Leonard Weisgard: Exponent of Beauty." *Elementary English* 47 (November, 1970): 922–935.

Covers details of his life, with quotations, and his training in the arts. Discusses many of his books, how they happened to be done, and gives analysis of the art in many of them plus some criticism of the quality of his work in general. A very useful discussion in more depth than most. Small b & w illustrations.

395.   ———. "Little Toot—Hero." *Elementary English* 37 (October, 1960): 363–367.

B & w photo portrait, one illustration. Brief summary of Gramatky's life, sketchy attempt to analyze the illustrations in a few paragraphs.

396.   ———. "Lynd Ward: Artist, Writer, and Scholar." *Elementary English* 39 (November, 1962): 663–671.

B & w photo portrait and some b & w illustrations. Brief summary of his life and success as an artist. Discussion of the relationship between his research and his illustration, and analysis of the emotional impact of some of the illustrations in a few books.

397.   ———, and Ulla Hyde Parker. *Cousin Beatie: A Memory of Beatrix Potter*. London: Warne, 1981. 40pp.

B & w and color illustrations and photographs. Personal reminiscences of what Beatrix Potter was like, with mention of the relationship of her art and her picture books.

398.   Perry, Erma. "The Gentle World of Ezra Jack Keats." *American Artist* 35 (September, 1971): 48–53, 71–73.

Illustrated in b & w and color, also photo portrait. Many quotes from Keats help describe the technique and materials used, how he works, and where he finds ideas. Notes on his life and hard times before attaining success.

399.   Porte, Barbara Ann. "The Picture Books of M.B. Goffstein." *Children's Literature in Education* 11, no. 1 (Spring, 1980): 3–9.

Mainly about the "story"; paragraph on p. 5 describes illustrations.

400. *Robert McCloskey.* (16mm color film.) (Videocassette.) Weston, Connecticut: Weston Woods, no date. 18 min.

The artist discusses the influences on his work, in his Maine studio and in the other places that have inspired him.

401. Rollin, Lucy. "The Astonished Witness Disclosed: An Interview with Arnold Lobel." *Children's Literature in Education* 15, no. 4 (Winter, 1984): 191–197.

Includes his reasons for drawing animal rather than people main characters. Covers his early development and mentions current work.

402. Sadowski, Eloise. "Glimpses of an Artist: Adrienne Adams." *Elementary English* 51 (October, 1974): 933–939.

Facts of her life plus a detailed description of how she works on a book from start to finish, including mention of her techniques for different books and details of her color separation work and use of the Dinobase process. List of her books and awards, photo portrait.

403. *Sendak.* (16 mm color film.) (Videocassette.) Weston, Connecticut: Weston Woods, 1987. 27 min.

The artist himself describes some events of his life and how they have influenced his work.

404. Sendak, Maurice. "The Aliveness of Peter Rabbit." *Wilson Library Bulletin* 40 (December, 1965): 345–348.

In a speech answering critics of Potter's *Peter Rabbit* and other such works for children, Sendak gives an enthusiastic and detailed analysis of her illustrations and technique along with an appreciation of the story.

405. ———. "Picture Book Genesis: A Conversation with Maurice Sendak." *Proceedings of the Fifth Annual Conference of the*

Children's Literature Association, Harvard University (March, 1978): 29–40.

Discusses the background and influences upon several of his works, including *Outside Over There, Some Swell Pup, Animal Family, Really Rosie*. His disgust with television for children, and the influence of music on his work are also touched upon.

406. Sleator, William. "An Illustrator Talks." *Publishers Weekly* 195 (February 17, 1969): 126–128.

This interview with Blair Lent asks a range of questions. Lent bases his answers on his belief that "the picturebook *can* be an art form," depending on how well the picture and the text work together. His art has evolved as print technology has made it possible to free himself from color separations. He believes that illustrating children's books is vital because the readers of them are at their most impressionable age.

407. Spencer, Isobel. *Walter Crane*. New York: Macmillan, 1975. 208pp.

Detailed account of his life and work includes his illustration, especially the chapter "Colour work for Edmund Evans: Yellow Backs and Toy Books," pp. 39–63, and "Illustration up to 1890," pp. 76–100, which also discusses his contemporaries, including Greenaway and Caldecott.

408. Spielmann, M.H., and G.S. Layard. *Kate Greenaway*. New York: Benjamin Blom, 1968 (reissue of 1905 edition). 300pp.

Many facsimile sketches and notes from her letters. Pages 265–284, "The Artist: A Review and an Estimate," analyze her work.

* *Story of a Book*. (Sound Filmstrip.) Holling C. Holling's *Pagoo*. Cited above as item 94.

409. Stott, John C. "Profile: Paul Goble." *Language Arts* 61 (December, 1984): 867–873.

In an interview Goble tells about his background, how he arrived in the U.S. and became interested in Native American culture, some individual books, and his life today. Some notes on the art and iconography. B & w portrait and illustrations.

410. Swanson, Mary T. *From Swedish Fairy Tales to American Fantasy. Gustaf Tenggren's Illustrations 1920–1970.* Minneapolis: University of Minnesota, 1986. 22pp.

Catalog of an exhibition from the University Art Museum. Discusses Tenggren's life and analyzes his work. Includes a chronology, a checklist of the works in the exhibition, and many b & w illustrations.

411. Swinger, Alice K. "Profile: Ashley Bryan." *Language Arts* 61 (March, 1984): 305–311.

A description of Bryan in his role as storyteller to an audience, notes on his life, and Bryan's own description of how he works to gather his words and to produce his images. Some discussion of individual books. Bibliography, b & w photos and illustration.

412. Taylor, Judy. *Beatrix Potter: Artist, Storyteller and Countrywoman.* New York: Warne/Viking Penguin, 1986. 224pp.

Many b & w illustrations and photographs, 28 color plates of her work. A very complete study of her life with details of her works. Little analysis of the pictures, however.

413. ———. *That Naughty Rabbit: Beatrix Potter and Peter Rabbit.* New York: Warne, 1987. 96pp.

A sympathetic and complete story of the genesis and evolution of *Peter Rabbit* from an illustrated letter to foreign translations and a myriad bits of merchandise (dolls, games, plates, napkins, etc.). Artistic and commercial details make this a particularly insightful analysis of the broader contemporary field of picturebook publishing.

414. *Tomi Ungerer: Storyteller.* (16mm color film.) (Videocassette.) Weston, Connecticut: Weston Woods, no date. 21 min.

The artist talks about his life and work and why he does controversial books. Scenes from the animated versions of his work are included.

415. Van Stockum, Hilda. "Caldecott's Pictures in Motion." *Horn Book* 22 (March–April, 1946): 119–125.

An artist's appreciative analysis of how Caldecott achieves a sense of motion in his illustrations, with b & w examples.

416. Waugh, Dorothy. "Adrienne Adams, Illustrator of Children's Books." *American Artist* 29 (November, 1965): 54–59, 74–75.

Many b & w illustrations. A very detailed analysis of her technique for both b & w and color illustrations, including the color separation process. Some notes on her life, her working method from receipt of manuscript through printing, and quotes from the artist.

417. ———. "Nonny Hogrogian, Decorator of Books for Children." *American Artist* 30 (October, 1966): 52–57.

Many examples of her woodcut illustrations. Detailed descriptions of her technique of making the woodblocks. Notes on some of her books and her life.

 * Weinstein, Frederic D. *Walter Crane and the American Book Arts, 1888–1915.* Cited above as item 69.

418. Wells, Rosemary. "The Artist at Work: The Writer at Work." *Horn Book* 63, no. 2 (March–April, 1987): 163–170.

Wells tells how and where she works, how she began illustrating, where some ideas have come from, why she uses animal characters, and the relationship of story and illustration.

419. Weston, Annette H. "Robert Lawson: Author and Illustrator." *Elementary English* 47, no. 1 (January, 1970): 74–84.

   B & w portrait photograph, biographical sketch, how he came to do some of his books, with quotations from the artist. Evaluation, pp. 82–83, includes discussion of his art.

420. White, Colin. *Edmund Dulac.* New York: Scribner's, 1976. 205pp.

   181 illustrations, 32 in color. Summary of his life and work. Illustrations for children not specified or analyzed separately.

421. White, David E. "A Conversation with Maurice Sendak." *Horn Book* 56 (April, 1980): 145–155.

   Discusses *Outside Over There*, the role of picture books for children and adults, Sendak's opinion of other picture books, and his current and future life plans.

422. _____. "Profile: Trina Schart Hyman." *Language Arts* 60 (September, 1983): 782–792.

   Mainly Hyman's own words on her life and the reasoning behind some of her illustrations, including the controversial. Very illuminating and informative. Partial bibliography of her works year by year. B & w photo portrait and illustrations.

423. White, Gabriel. *Edward Ardizzone: Artist and Illustrator.* New York: Schocken, 1979. 191pp.

   Profusely illustrated on every page with b & w and six color page illustrations. After a brief summary of Ardizzone's childhood, early life in London and start as an illustrator, White concentrates his comments on the work and a critical appraisal of style.

424. Wildsmith, Brian. "Antic Disposition: A Young Illustrator Interviews Himself." *Library Journal* 90 (November, 1965):

5035–5038 and *School Library Journal* 12 (November, 1965): 21–24.

B & w photo portrait and illustrations. In a question-and-answer format the illustrator sums up his life, how he came to illustration, especially for children, and a bit about his aims as illustrator.

425. Wilkens, Lea-Ruth C. "Walter Crane and the Reform of the German Picture Book, 1865–1914." Pittsburgh: University of Pittsburgh, 1973. University Microfilm No. 74–1452. 138pp.

Discusses how Crane's work was a catalyst in Germany. Two major exhibitions have been organized by German teachers' organizations to show this.

426. Wood, Don, and Audrey Wood. "The Artist at Work: Where Ideas Come From." *Horn Book* 62, no. 5 (September–October, 1986): 556–565.

The Woods describe the origins of several of their books and how the art and text work together toward the final product. B & w examples.

427. Yorinks, Arthur. "Richard Egielski." *Horn Book* 63, no. 4 (July–August, 1987): 436–438.

His collaborator's brief view and appreciation of Egielski's life and work.

428. Zemach, Margot. *Self-Portrait: Margot Zemach.* Reading, Massachusetts: Addison-Wesley, 1978. 31pp.

Profusely illustrated by the author. Zemach tells the story of her life very simply, from childhood on. She does not discuss her art, but it covers the pages.

429. _____, and Harve Zemach. "Profile of an Author and an Illustrator." *Top of the News* 27 (April, 1971): 248–255.

In answering questions, Margot Zemach briefly fills in her background, and on pp. 251–252 talks about how she came to, and feels about, illustration. Their collaboration is also covered.

430. Zuckerman, Linda. "Don Freeman: An Editor's View." *Horn Book* 54 (June, 1979): 273–281.

The editor's view of her relationship with Freeman and how they worked together. Includes his account of how he "found" the stories for the Corduroy books, and notes on his artwork for picture books and that done for galleries.

PART VI

Guides and Aids to Further Research

* Beach, Barbara, ed. *Children's Book Review Index.* Cited below as item 432.

431. Best, James J. *American Popular Illustration: A Reference Guide.* Westport, Connecticut: Greenwood, 1984. 171pp.

Covers historic background, major illustrated works and their illustrators, the social and artistic content, and techniques, with introductory notes to each section. Works on children's picture books are included but must be searched out. Appendix 3, pp. 157–162, is a bibliography of illustrated books by author.

* Brenni, Vito J., compiler. *Book Illustration and Decoration: A Guide to Research.* Cited above as item 12.

432. *Children's Book Review Index.* Detroit: Gale, annual since 1975.

Cites all reviews of children's books (grades K–5) appearing in this publisher's *Book Review Index.* More than 460 periodicals are currently indexed, over 100 of which review children's books. The arrangement is alphabetical by author. In earlier volumes, the illustrator's name is listed with the title. Beginning with the 1986 annual, there is also an index of illustrators.

433. *Children's Books: Awards and Prizes.* New York: Children's Book Council. Revised biennially.

A listing of the prizes and their winners in the U.S. and the British Commonwealth with some international awards included. Illustrators are named only when the awards are specifically for illustration or design. In Appendix A, "Awards Classified," is a list of awards for illustration or design. Illustrators can be found in the index of persons.

434. Davis, Dorothy R., ed. *The Carolyn Sherwin Bailey Historical Collection of Children's Books: A Catalog.* New Haven: South Connecticut State College, 1966. 232pp.

Some b & w illustrations. From the 3000 books, games and items in this collection, 1880 are listed. The books were published in Great Britain and the U.S. from 1657.

435. Ellis, Alec. *How to Find Out About Children's Literature.* New York: Pergamon, 2nd ed., 1968. 3rd ed., 1973. 252pp.

Includes chapters on the growing importance of children's literature, purpose in children's reading, reading and child development. Details search strategies. Bibliographies must be searched by name of individual illustrator. Pages 104–105 list British and international periodicals that include articles on illustrators. Includes list of Kate Greenaway winners, 1955–1971.

436. Ettlinger, John R.T., and Diana Spirt. *Choosing Books for Young People: A Guide to Criticism and Bibliography 1945–1975.* Chicago: American Library Association, 1982. 219pp.

An alphabetical annotated listing. Relevant sources must be found under "Illustration" and "Illustrators." Volume 2, 1976–1984, 168pp., has just been published by Oryx Press.

437. Hannabuss, Stuart. "Sources of Information for Children's Book Illustration." *Journal of Librarianship* 13, no. 3 (July, 1981): 154–171.

Many sources including British are listed, unfortunately in paragraph form making retrieval very difficult. Appreciative comments for the researcher.

438. Haviland, Virginia, and Margaret N. Coughlan, compilers. *Children's Literature: A Guide to Reference Sources.* Washington, D.C.: Library of Congress, 1966. First Supplement 1972. Second Supplement 1977. Pages vary.

Some b & w illustrations included. These comprehensive annotated bibliographies cover all areas of children's literature. Of particular relevance to picture books are "Illustrating for Children," pp. 77–83 in the first supplement and pp. 109–117 in the second supplement; and "Critical Appraisals of Individual Illustrators," pp. 83–87 in the first supplement and pp. 117–125 in the second supplement. Sources on history and collections are also included.

439. Hendrickson, Linnea. *Children's Literature: A Guide to the Criticism.* Boston: G.K. Hall, 1987. 664pp.

Includes articles, books and dissertations from a wide range of sources, emphasizing the 20th century. Part A, "Authors and Their Works," pp. 1–298, includes many illustrators in the alphabetical listing of subjects. Part B, "Subjects, Themes, and Genres," includes lists of sources under relevant subjects such as "Alphabet Books," pp. 306–307; "Art," p. 311; "Picture Books," pp. 477–495; "Toy Books," p. 553; "Wordless Picture Books," pp. 507–571.

There is an index of critics as well as of authors, titles and subjects. Other subjects with references in the index include: Children's preferences in picture books, Fairy and folktale illustration, Abstract illustrations, Continuity in illustrations, Endpaper illustration, Photographic illustration, Scratchboard illustration, Woodcut illustration, Picture book evaluation and reader response, and names of individual illustrators. This incredibly comprehensive work also covers British periodicals unavailable to the compilers of this bibliography.

440. *The Kerlan Collection: Manuscripts and Illustrations for Children's Books.* Minneapolis: University of Minnesota, 1984. 432pp.

A checklist of the manuscripts and/or illustrations for over 4,950 books that are in the collection from 640 authors and/or 584 illustrators and 31 translators. Indexed by author, title, translator, illustrator, editor and subject.

441. Lief, Irving P. *Children's Literature: A Historical and Contemporary Bibliography.* Troy, New York: Whitston, 1977. 338pp.

Has sections on trends in various countries, on identifying old editions, old school books, and on authors, with listings of unpublished theses and magazine articles as well as books. "Children's Book Illustration" section includes: "The Art of Illustrated Children's Books," pp. 249–256; "Picture books," pp. 256–259; "Illustrators of Children's Books" and "General Biographies and critiques," pp. 259–261. Individual illustrators, pp. 261–297. Many foreign illustrators, also authors and references in non-english languages.

442. Meacham, Mary. *Information Sources in Children's Literature: A Practical Reference Guide for Children's Librarians, Elementary School Teachers, and Students of Children's Literature.* Westport, Connecticut: Greenwood, 1978. 256pp.

The chapter "Illustrators, Authors and Awards" (pp. 198–201) covers illustrators.

443. Monson, Diane, and Bette J. Peltola, compilers. *Research in Children's Literature: An Annotated Bibliography.* Newark, Delaware: International Reading Association, 1976. 96pp.

Index enables one to find articles on "Caldecott," "Illustrators," and "Picture storybook." Many entries on using these books for reading purposes. Dissertations, journal articles, related studies and ERIC documents are included.

444. Nakamura, Joyce, ed. *Children's Authors and Illustrators: An Index to Biographical Dictionaries.* 4th ed. Detroit: Gale, 1987. 799pp.

More that 450 reference sources are indexed in this update of the series formerly edited by Sarkissian. Entries from previous editions have been updated, and pseudonyms and other name variants are included.

* Pellowski, Anne. *The World of Children's Literature.* Cited above as item 51.

445. Peterson, Linda Kauffman, and Marilyn Leathers Solt. *Newbery and Caldecott Medal and Honor Books: An Annotated Bibliography.* Boston: G.K. Hall, 1982. 427pp.

Includes history of the medals, notes on characteristics and trends. Each book listed with summary and critical commentary. Complete list to 1981. Appendix: terms, definitions, criteria, pp. 399–401.

446. Provenzo, Eugene F., Jr. "A Note on the Darton Collection." *Teacher's College Record* 84 (Summer, 1983): 929–934.

Describes contents of the collection.

447. Quimby, Harriet B., with Margaret Mary Kimmel. *Building a Children's Literature Collection: A Suggested Basic Reference Collection for Academic Libraries and a Suggested Basic Collection of Children's Books.* 3rd ed. Middletown, Connecticut: Choice, 1983. 48pp. Bibliographic Essay Series, No. 7.

Lists general texts, histories, sources on authors, specific picture book sources pp. 3–4, critical works, awards and prizes, international sources, other areas of interest, including books on parenting and how to write for children and young people. Lists include books by area (picture books, pp. 21–23) and both author and title indexes.

448. Rahn, Suzanne. *Children's Literature: An Annotated Bibliography of the History and Criticism.* New York: Garland, 1981. 451pp.

Books about picture books and their creators can be found in the section "Studies of Genres" in "Books for Children Under Five," pp. 78–80, with references to specific people in the later section on individual authors.

* Roginski, James W. *Newbery and Caldecott Medalists and Honor Book Winners: Bibliographies and Resource Material Through 1977.* Cited above as item 290.

449. Sarkissian, Adele, ed. *Children's Authors and Illustrators: An Index to Biographical Dictionaries.* 3rd ed. Detroit: Gale, 1981. 2nd ed. 1978, 667pp.

More than 250 reference sources for biographical information are indexed in alphabetical order by name of author or illustrator followed by birth and death date and code letters for the sources of information. Includes list of titles indexed with abbreviations. For fourth edition, 1987, see Nakamura, Joyce (item 444, above).

450. St. John, Judith. *The Osborne Collection of Early Children's Books 1566–1910: A Catalogue.* Toronto: Toronto Public Library, 1958. 561pp.

Reprinted 1975. Illustrated with many b & w examples of title pages and book illustrations and 12 color plates. The catalogue lists the books by types including "Nursery rhymes and alphabets" and "Movable and toy books." There is a list of illustrators and engravers.

451. _____. *The Osborne Collection of Early Children's Books 1476–1910: A Catalogue.* Toronto: Toronto Public Library, 1975. Vol. 2, pp. 563–1138.

Includes some small b & w illustrations. Books are listed by types as in Volume One, but there is no index of illustrators or engravers.

* Tarbert, Gary C., ed. *Children's Book Review Index.* Cited above as item 432.

* Woolman, Bertha. *The Caldecott Award: The Winners and the Honor Books.* Cited above as item 298.

PART VII

Some Collections and/or Repositories of Materials on Picture Books and their Creators

Alice M. Jordon Collection. Boston Public Library, Boston, Massachusetts.

A children's literature research collection that includes, in addition to print materials, correspondences, memorabilia, taped interviews, videotapes, etc.

Babbidge Library Special Collections Department. University of Connecticut, Storrs, Connecticut.

Includes a recently donated collection of over 5,000 illustrated books and the original art work by Richard Scarry for 27 of his books.

Beinecke Library. Yale University, New Haven, Connecticut.

Some illustrations along with many manuscripts, letters, etc., of authors and illustrators of children's books.

Carolyn Sherwin Bailey Historical Collection of Children's Books. Southern Connecticut State College, New Haven, Connecticut.

About 3000 books and some other items from the early 17th century onwards.

Darton Collection. Teachers College, Columbia University, New York City.

> Collection includes 1400 titles, some English children's books published before 1850, a 1763 Newbery publication, pedagogical and other board games, scrapbooks, original sketches and watercolors by Kate Greenaway and others.

De Grummond Collection. University of Southern Mississippi.

> "Largest collection of original children's literature material in the U.S."

Donnell Branch, New York Public Library, New York City.

> Early illustrated books and some original art for picture books.

Gail E. Haley Collection of the Culture of Childhood. Appalachian State University, Boone, North Carolina.

> Includes games, toys, books, dolls, puppets and other artifacts from many countries and cultures. Some of the linocuts, woodblocks, sketches and finished artwork for Gail Haley's book are also here.

Kerlan Collection. University of Minnesota, Minneapolis, Minnesota.

> More than 4950 books are represented by manuscripts and/or illustrations donated by 640 authors and/or illustrators and 31 translators, all of which document the stages in the production of the books.

Library of Congress Special Collection, Washington, D.C.

> Some rare children's books, including some illustrated books.

Mary Faulk Markiewicz Collection of Early American Children's Books. University of Rochester, Rochester, New York.

More than 1,000 volumes, mainly for older children, but includes some picture books and alphabet books.

May Massee Collection. Emporia State University, Emporia, Kansas.

Morgan Library. New York City.

Many children's books, including early illustrated books.

The Osborne Collection of Early Children's Books. Toronto Public Library, Toronto, Canada.

Several thousand books plus games, periodicals, toy books, etc., from the last 400 years in England were donated by Edgar Osborne in 1949. The collection has been augmented by purchases and donations since.

Rosenbach Collection. Free Library of Philadelphia, Pennsylvania.

A collection of rare children's books.

INDEX OF ARTISTS

INDEX OF AUTHORS, EDITORS AND COMPILERS

INDEX OF TITLES